BOUNTIFUL BOWLS

BOUNTIFUL BOWLS

FRESH, VIBRANT AND NUTRITIOUS FLAVOURS IN A BOWL

CONTENTS

THE POWER OF THE BOWL

THE POWER BOWL IS NOT A NEW PHENOMENON. MANY CULTURES HAVE STRONG BOWL FOOD TRADITIONS, RANGING FROM THE NORTHERN EUROPEAN BOWL OF PORRIDGE TO THE KOREAN RICE DISH *BIBIMBAP*.

The recent popularity of eating from a bowl has its roots in America in the noughties, with New York salad restaurant chains such as Sweetgreen and Liquiteria offering meals in a bowl as part of a mission to provide seasonal, healthy food in a fresh, appealing, no-nonsense way. This tuned in to the popular zeitgeist, and with a big boost from food bloggers and social media, the bowl trend made an impact on all those who wanted a diet full of goodness. With their contents constantly reinvented, bowls continue to make their way into our kitchens.

Simply put, food looks incredibly appetizing in a bowl. It has impact. It's certainly easy to eat – all you need is a fork and a variety of small or chopped ingredients that can be speared and munched easily. Food in a bowl also gives you flexibility. It's so simple to eat your meal informally – you can cradle a warming bowl in your hands as you chat to friends, or relax in the garden on a hot day with an easy salad bowl.

It's not just about the bowl. The power of the formula is that a bowl can be filled with a healthy combination of colourful fruit and vegetables, lean protein and great-tasting dressings, with a sprinkling of superfoods such as shredded kale, grated carrot, alfalfa sprouts or sunflower seeds to round it off.

Power bowls, invariably full of colour and bursting with healthy ingredients, are highly photogenic

(this is why they look so appetizing), and they have spread their allure on social media channels as people share their healthy and appetising bowls on food blogs and platforms such as Twitter and Instagram.

Bowls also break away from the predictable formula of recipes that serve four. That's fine if you are preparing a family meal, but what about if you live alone, want to eat at a different time, or just want to eat alone? Bowls allow you to escape from the traditional formulas of meals on a plate – ingredients are driven by fruit, vegetables, high protein content and a rainbow of colours.

Power bowls are so named to explain the power punch of superfoods and nutrients that they offer, which will help to keep you energized throughout the day. While there are no rules – you can use ingredients you really love to fit any cuisine or taste – there are certain types of bowls that have become popular.

Smoothie bowls are a delicious addition to the breakfast table, and can also be served as a dessert. Examples here are the Summer Melon Bowl on page 26 or the Strawberry & Rhubarb Smoothie Bowl on page 164.

Breakfast bowls break away from the standard breakfast routine of cereal and milk, adding ingredients that will increase the nutritional value and the visual appeal of your first meal of the

day. Examples here are the Fruity Sweet Potato Breakfast Bowl on page 42 and the Bubble & Squeak Breakfast Bowl on page 40.

Buddha bowls, also referred to as sunshine or glory bowls, are named after the traditional nested Buddha bowls or *oryoki* used by Buddhist monks. These meatless meals for one are filling bowls of raw or roasted vegetables, beans, healthy grains such as quinoa or brown rice and lots of greens. Toppings may include nuts or seeds and a drizzle of dressing. Why not try the Summer Abundance Salad on page 88 or the Harissa Veggie Bowl on page 112?

Poke bowls (pronounced *poh-keh*), meaning 'slice and cut', are based on a traditional Hawaiian dish, which was originally just delicious raw fish and rice, a bit like deconstructed sushi, seasoned to taste. They have now evolved to include cooked fish, salad ingredients and seeds (see the Tuna Poke Bowl on page 72).

Bowls also offer a great choice for specific diets. Most of the bowls here cater for vegetarian, vegan, gluten-free, dairy-free and raw diets, and are identified with a key (see page 9). Examples include the Vegetable Rice Bowl on page 54, the Lentil & Amaranth Tabbouleh on page 124 and the Quinoa Fruit Salad on page 152.

Another attraction is the sheer simplicity of preparing a bowl. All the recipe bowls here are generally simple to put together. They use fresh ingredients that are chopped, grated, roasted or blended, and some that are cooked or steamed, to create great texture, with the addition of spices and herbs for flavour.

CREATING NUTRITIONAL BALANCE

The key to eating a balanced and nutritious diet is variety. We all need basic micronutrients for optimum health – carbohydrates for energy, proteins for muscle repair and the immune system, and essential fats for brain and cell health. To help the body to break down the micronutrients, large amounts of macronutrients are needed – these are found in vitamins and minerals, and we get them principally from colourful fruits and vegetables. The traditional adage 'eat a rainbow every day' steers us towards a daily intake of a variety of nutrients – with bowl food you can make sure you have a rainbow in every bowl.

BOWL INGREDIENTS

FRUIT AND VEGETABLES

We all know we need to eat plenty of fruit and vegetables, at least five portions a day, most of which should be vegetables. Fruit and vegetables in different colours contain different vitamins, minerals and phytochemicals, which all help to keep you healthy. Eat fruit and vegetables that are in season, and source them locally if you can. You can chop, grate, roast or steam vegetables and plan to make them at least 50 per cent of your bowl. Avoid frying vegetables as cooking at high temperatures can have a detrimental affect on nutrients.

CEREALS, GRAINS, PASTA, RICE, NOODLES AND POTATOES

Foods in this group provide energy and dietary fibre, a range of vitamins, minerals and small amounts of protein. Choose wholegrain varieties, such as brown rice, wholemeal pasta and unrefined cereals, to keep your digestive system and heart healthy. Quinoa, brown rice and noodles are all quick and nutritious and make a good base for other ingredients. These are great carbohydrate foods, important for energy.

PROTEIN

Protein is essential for growth and the repair of cells. It also provides essential vitamins and minerals. It is wise to aim for 70–150 g/2½–5½ oz protein with each meal. You can use fish, chicken, red meat, seafood, eggs or cheese for your protein allowance. While dairy products are high in protein, non-dairy milk, yogurt and cheese, other than soya, have a low protein load. Vegetarians and vegans can combine grains and pulses, such as rice, quinoa, lentils and beans, to get a full protein boost. Tofu works well with the addition of tasty spices and dressings.

HEALTHY UNSATURATED FATS

We need fat in our diet to help the body to absorb fat-soluble vitamins A, D, E and K and to provide essential fatty acids. These are found in oily fish such as salmon, mackerel, herring and fresh tuna, and in plant products such as olive oil, flaxseed oil, avocados, pecan nuts and pumpkin seeds. When planning your bowl, aim to include around 10 per cent healthy unsaturated fat.

HERBS

Herbs add great flavour to a wide range of dishes and many have therapeutic qualities too. Turmeric, for example, is a natural anti-inflammatory, mint helps aid digestion and ginger also supports the digestive system.

Planning ahead will help you with your bowl preparation. Certain things can be made in bulk – dressings prepared in advance can be stored in the refrigerator, and chutneys and pickles made with fresh seasonal ingredients can be bottled and stored until needed. Fruit purées can be frozen in ice cube trays. Other foods that can be made in advance include roasted vegetables, hummus, overnight oats, baked sweet potatoes and coleslaw.

Whatever your food preferences, the power-bowl formula is a simple and dramatic way to serve up delicious food that is packed with nutrition.

KEY

GLUTEN-FREE · VEGETARIAN · DAIRY-FREE · RAW · VEGAN

The coloured icons included with the recipes throughout the book indicate those that suit specific diets: vegetarian, gluten-free, dairy-free, raw and vegan. This will be a useful guide if you follow any of these diets, or if you are preparing food for friends and family who follow a diet.

BREAKFAST

TURMERIC & CHIA OVERNIGHT OATS

TURMERIC HAS AN INGREDIENT CALLED CURCUMIN, A POWERFUL ANTI-INFLAMMATORY AND A STRONG ANTIOXIDANT, SO THIS BREAKFAST DISH IS A HEALTHY WAY TO START THE DAY.

 10 mins, plus chilling 5 mins 2

INGREDIENTS

100 g/3½ oz rolled oats

grated zest of 1 orange

400 ml/14 fl oz fresh orange juice

¼ tsp ground turmeric

1 tbsp chia seeds

100 g/3½ oz strawberries, hulled and sliced

40 g/1½ oz blueberries

60 g/2¼ oz raspberries

1 tbsp pomegranate seeds

2 tsp desiccated coconut

1. Place the oats in a medium-sized saucepan.

2. Whisk together the orange zest, 300 ml/10 fl oz of the orange juice and the turmeric. Pour the mixture over the oats and cook, stirring, over a low heat for 4–5 minutes.

3. Remove from the heat and stir in the remaining orange juice and the chia seeds. Divide between two bowls and chill in the refrigerator overnight.

4. When ready to serve top each bowl with the strawberries, blueberries, raspberries, pomegranate seeds and desiccated coconut.

This recipe could also be served warm, topped with warming stewed fruits such as plums or rhubarb, with perhaps a dollop of natural yogurt.

PER SERVING : 399 KCALS | 9.1G FAT | 2.6G SAT FAT | 73.1G CARBS | 24.6G SUGAR | 13G FIBRE | 10.8G PROTEIN | TRACE SALT

COCONUT POWER BOWL

THIS RECIPE USES A DELICIOUS HOMEMADE QUINOA GRANOLA, WHICH IS RICHER IN PROTEIN AND LOWER IN SUGAR THAN MOST SHOP-BOUGHT GRANOLAS.

INGREDIENTS

100 g/3½ oz coconut oil

1 tbsp honey

2 tbsp dark muscovado sugar

100 g/3½ oz quinoa flakes

150 g/5½ oz rolled oats

3 tbsp desiccated coconut

½ tsp ground cinnamon

1 tbsp dried cranberries

1 tbsp chopped pecan nuts

2 bananas, peeled and chopped

55 g/2 oz walnuts

200 ml/7 fl oz coconut milk

1 tsp ground cinnamon

100 g/3½ oz raspberries

10 g/¼ oz fresh mint leaves

2 tbsp maple syrup

1. Preheat the oven to 180°C/350°F/Gas Mark 4. Put the coconut oil, honey and sugar into a saucepan over a low heat and heat, stirring, until the sugar has dissolved.

2. Remove from the heat and stir in the quinoa flakes, 55 g/ 2 oz of the oats, 2 tablespoons of the desiccated coconut, the cinnamon, cranberries and pecan nuts. Mix well to combine.

3. Spread the mixture over a baking sheet and bake in the preheated oven for 15 minutes, stirring halfway through the cooking time.

4. Remove from the oven, spoon into a bowl and leave to cool.

5. Meanwhile, place the bananas, the remaining oats, the walnuts and coconut milk in a food processor and process until almost smooth.

6. Pour into four bowls and add the granola. Top with the cinnamon, raspberries, mint, the remaining desiccated coconut, and a drizzle of maple syrup.

PER SERVING : 43.1 KCALS | 43.1G FAT | 26G SAT FAT | 84.7G CARBS | 31.3G SUGAR | 11.3G FIBRE | 11.8G PROTEIN | 0.1G SALT

BLUEBERRY PORRIDGE PIE

HERE'S A DELICIOUS, FIBRE-RICH PORRIDGE PACKED WITH FRUIT AND TOPPED WITH A SWEET, STICKY AND CRUNCHY CRUMBLE. EVERYONE WILL LOVE THIS!

15 mins, plus soaking

None

INGREDIENTS

85 g/3 oz raw rolled oats

1½ tsp chia seeds

2½ tbsp raw dried coconut flakes

¾ tsp ground cinnamon

1 banana, peeled and roughly chopped

juice of ¼ lemon

1¾ tbsp raw honey

60 g/2¼ oz blueberries

225 ml/8 fl oz raw coconut milk

2 tbsp chopped raw almonds

½ tbsp milled flaxseed

1 tbsp sunflower seeds

1. Combine the oats, chia seeds, 2 tablespoons of the coconut flakes and half a teaspoon of the cinnamon in a mixing bowl.

2. Put the banana pieces in a small bowl. Sprinkle over the lemon juice and stir in 1 tablespoon of the honey, making sure each piece of banana is coated with the mixture. (You can warm the honey slightly if it's too solid to stir in.)

3. Stir the bananas, half the blueberries and the coconut milk into the oat mixture and combine. Spoon evenly into two serving bowls, pressing the banana pieces into the porridge. Cover the bowls with clingfilm or foil and leave in the refrigerator overnight.

4. Meanwhile, start making the pie topping. In a small bowl, stir the almonds, flaxseed and sunflower seeds together. Stir in the remaining cinnamon and honey, warmed if necessary. Mix thoroughly and leave covered for the morning.

5. Before serving, sprinkle the topping over the porridge and decorate with the remaining coconut flakes and blueberries.

While the porridge tastes great served cold, it can also be warmed gently to 40°C/104°F before you add the topping.

PER SERVING : 582 KCALS | 29.6G FAT | 17.1G SAT FAT | 75G CARBS | 29.4G SUGAR | 14.6G FIBRE | 12G PROTEIN | TRACE SALT

CREAMY RICOTTA BREAKFAST BOWL

A LIGHT, CREAMY BREAKFAST THAT IS PERFECT FOR A SUMMER MORNING.
TOP IT WITH SEASONAL FRUITS OF YOUR CHOICE.

INGREDIENTS

200 g/7 oz ricotta cheese

grated rind of ½ orange

grated rind of 1 lemon

1 mango, peeled, stoned and sliced

2 blood oranges, peeled and sliced

1 passion fruit, halved, flesh only

1 tbsp gluten-free granola

1–2 tsp honey (optional)

1. Place the ricotta cheese in a medium-sized bowl and stir through the grated orange rind and lemon rind.

2. Divide the mixture between two smaller bowls.

3. Top with the mango slices, blood orange slices and passion fruit flesh, then sprinkle over the granola and honey, if using, and serve immediately.

You may want to omit the honey and sprinkle with ground cinnamon instead – this is a great way of adding flavour, and cinnamon is also is known to help control blood sugar levels.

PER SERVING : 369 KCALS | 15.5G FAT | 8.7G SAT FAT | 38.6G CARBS | 23.8G SUGAR | 9.3G FIBRE | 14.8G PROTEIN | 0.2G SALT

ACAI & BERRY MORNING JAR

AFTER CHILLING THIS BREAKFAST JAR IN THE REFRIGERATOR OVERNIGHT, ALL YOU NEED TO DO IS POP THE TOPPING ON FOR BREAKFAST – OR, INDEED, ANY MEAL OF THE DAY!

10 mins, plus resting and chilling

None

INGREDIENTS

90 g/3¼ oz strawberries

90 g/3¼ oz raspberries

35 g/1¼ oz blueberries

150 g/5½ oz raw coconut yogurt (see recipe below)

50 ml/2 fl oz raw coconut milk

½ tsp vanilla pod seeds

1 tbsp chia seeds

2 tsp raw honey

1 tsp acai powder

½ tbsp lemon juice

2 tbsp raw cashew nut butter

1 tsp hemp seeds

2 fresh mint sprigs

RAW COCONUT YOGURT

225 g/8 oz fresh or frozen coconut meat, thawed if frozen

100 ml/3½ fl oz raw coconut water

1 probiotic powder capsule

1. To make the coconut yogurt, blend the coconut meat and coconut water in a blender until smooth. Empty the powder from the probiotic capsule into the mixture and blend again for a few seconds.

2. Pour the coconut mixture into a bowl, cover with clingfilm or foil, and leave in the kitchen overnight at warm room temperature. In the morning, you should have about 300 g/ 10½ oz yogurt. Remove what you need and the rest will keep in the refrigerator for up to a week.

3. Blend 70 g/2½ oz strawberries, 70 g/2½ oz raspberries and 30 g/1 oz blueberries with the yogurt, coconut milk, vanilla seeds, chia seeds, honey, acai powder and lemon juice until smooth. Pour the mixture into a wide-necked jar with a 300–325 ml/ 10–11 fl oz capacity. Cover and chill in the refrigerator overnight.

4. The following morning, top with the cashew butter and the remaining berries, followed by the hemp seeds and mint sprigs.

Chia seeds can be used to thicken smoothies and desserts. They also provide essential vitamins, minerals and omega-3 fats.

PER SERVING : 897 KCALS | 67.3G FAT | 42.7G SAT FAT | 72.1G CARBS | 34.6G SUGAR | 26.9G FIBRE | 15.4G PROTEIN | 0.1G SALT

PEAR, BANANA & APPLE BREAKFAST BOWL

IF YOU'RE TIRED OF EATING GRAINS FOR BREAKFAST, THIS FRUITY BREAKFAST BOWL WILL INVIGORATE – IT'S FULL OF FRESH AUTUMNAL FLAVOURS, FIERY CINNAMON AND DELICIOUS DRIED BERRIES.

15 mins, plus optional chilling

  None

INGREDIENTS

2 ripe dessert pears

2 green-skinned apples, such as Granny Smith

1 large banana, peeled and chopped

75 ml/2½ fl oz apple juice

juice of ½ lemon

2 tbsp sultanas

2 tbsp raw cashew nuts

1 tbsp sunflower seeds

1 tbsp raw sugar

½ tsp ground cinnamon

1 tbsp goldenberries

1 tbsp cranberries

1. Core and chop one pear and one apple. Place them in a serving bowl with half the banana and pour over half the apple juice and half the lemon juice. Stir well to combine.

2. Core, peel and roughly chop the remaining pear and apple. Add them to a blender with the rest of the banana.

3. Add the remaining apple juice and lemon juice to the blender with the sultanas and nuts. Blend until you have a finely chopped mixture.

4. Stir the blended mixture into the chopped fruit, along with the sunflower seeds, sugar and cinnamon. Scatter over the goldenberries and cranberries. Chill in the refrigerator if you have time, or serve immediately.

Goldenberries are dried physalis – the small and tangy orange fruits you find for sale in late autumn.

PER SERVING : 438 KCALS | 7.5G FAT | 1G SAT FAT | 93.8G CARBS | 62.5G SUGAR | 5.5G FIBRE | 5.5G PROTEIN | TRACE SALT

VERY BERRY OVERNIGHT OATS

MADE IN A LIDDED JAR, THIS IS A PERFECT BREAKFAST TO BRING TO WORK. PREPARE YOUR OATS THE NIGHT BEFORE AND THEY'LL BE READY TO EAT OR PICK UP WITH NO FUSS IN THE MORNING.

15 mins, plus chilling | None | 1

INGREDIENTS

40 g/1½ oz raw rolled oats

½ tbsp milled flaxseed

½ tbsp acai berry powder

2 tsp goji berries

1 tbsp flaked almonds

½ tbsp raw honey

125 ml/4 fl oz raw almond milk

2 tbsp blueberries

3 strawberries

1. Put the oats, flaxseed, acai berry powder, goji berries, most of the flaked almonds, the honey and almond milk in a lidded jar with a 225–250 ml/8–9 fl oz capacity. Stir well.

2. Stir a few of the blueberries into the oat mixture. Close the jar and chill in the refrigerator overnight.

3. In the morning, chop the strawberries. Top the oats with the remaining blueberries, strawberries and the remaining almonds.

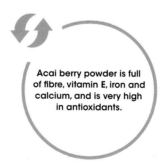

Acai berry powder is full of fibre, vitamin E, iron and calcium, and is very high in antioxidants.

PER SERVING : 437 KCALS | 21.5G FAT | 1.7G SAT FAT | 52.3G CARBS | 15.9G SUGAR | 11.1G FIBRE | 13.1G PROTEIN | TRACE SALT

SUMMER MELON BOWL

USING THE MELON AS A BOWL CREATES A UNIQUE VESSEL FOR A DELICIOUSLY FRUITY START TO THE DAY PACKED WITH THE TROPICAL TASTE OF COCONUT.

INGREDIENTS

1 cantaloupe melon, halved and seeds removed

150 g/5½ oz raspberries

2 kiwis, cubed

15 g/½ oz mint, roughly chopped

juice of 1 lime

1 tbsp coconut oil

60 g/2¼ oz oats

200 g/7 oz coconut yogurt, to serve

1. Using a large spoon, scoop the flesh from the melon, leaving the skin to create two melon 'bowls'. Cut the melon flesh into bite-sized chunks and transfer half of the chunks into a large bowl, reserving the remainder for another meal. Add the raspberries, kiwis, chopped mint and lime juice. Working very carefully, so as not to damage the fruit, combine. Set aside.

2. Heat a small frying pan over a medium heat and add the coconut oil. Heat until molten before adding the oats and continue to cook for 3–4 minutes until the oats have toasted.

3. Fill the bowls with the fresh fruit and scatter with oats. Serve with dollops of coconut yogurt.

PER SERVING : 496 KCALS | 21.6G FAT | 16.9G SAT FAT | 70.6G CARBS | 34.3G SUGAR | 13.2G FIBRE | 9.5G PROTEIN | 0.1G SALT

MORNING POWERBOWL SMOOTHIE

HERE'S A GREAT WAY TO INCREASE YOUR NUTRIENT INTAKE, WITH LOTS OF COLOURFUL FRUITS TO PROVIDE ANTIOXIDANTS, AND HEALTHY FATS FROM NUTS AND SEEDS.

10 mins, plus chilling

None

INGREDIENTS

50 g/1¾ oz strawberries

50 g/1¾ oz blackberries

50 g/1¾ oz raspberries

1 banana, peeled

150 ml/5 fl oz hemp milk

1 tbsp coconut oil

1 tbsp ground almonds

1 kiwi, peeled and sliced

2 tsp chia seeds

1 small mango, peeled, stoned and chopped

1 tbsp chopped walnuts

2 tsp toasted sesame seeds

1. Place the strawberries, blackberries, raspberries, half the banana, the hemp milk, coconut oil and ground almonds in a blender and blend until smooth.

2. Pour into a bowl and place the remaining ingredients on top to serve.

Replace the topping with fruits and nuts of your choice, aiming to use those in season – luscious berries would be great in the summer, sprinkled with freshly shredded mint leaves.

PER SERVING : 654 KCALS | 34.4G FAT | 13.8G SAT FAT | 86.9G CARBS | 51.1G SUGAR | 19.5G FIBRE | 11.1G PROTEIN | 0.1G SALT

LAYERED POWERBOWL SMOOTHIE

THE COMBINATION OF FLAVOURS IN THIS COLOURFUL SMOOTHIE IS DELICIOUS! RICH IN ANTIOXIDANTS FROM THE FRUITS AND PROTEIN FROM THE ALMONDS AND SESAME SEEDS, THIS IS A GREAT BREAKFAST.

INGREDIENTS

1 large mango, peeled and chopped

2 kiwi fruit, peeled and chopped

½ tsp chlorella powder

450 g/1 lb watermelon, peeled and chopped (leave the pips in for additional vitamins)

1 tbsp ground almonds

1 tsp sesame seeds

2 tbsp gluten-free granola

¼ tsp ground cinnamon

1. Place the mango in a small blender and process until smooth. Divide between two glass bowls. Rinse the blender.

2. Place the kiwi and chlorella powder in the blender and process until smooth. Spoon over the layer of mango in the bowls. Rinse the blender.

3. Place the watermelon in the blender and process until smooth. Add the ground almonds and sesame seeds and process briefly to combine. Spoon over the kiwi mixture.

4. Sprinkle with the granola and ground cinnamon and serve.

PER SERVING : 303 KCALS | 6.4G FAT | 1.1G SAT FAT | 61.3G CARBS | 44.2G SUGAR | 7.1G FIBRE | 6.4G PROTEIN | TRACE SALT

GRAPES, KIWI & SPINACH SMOOTHIE BOWL

THIS HEALTH-IN-A-BOWL DISH IS BURSTING WITH NUTRIENT-PACKED NUTS, VITAMIN-FILLED FRUITS AND LOTS OF GOODNESS. PERFECT AS A PICK ME UP OR AFTER A HEAVY MAIN MEAL.

INGREDIENTS

200 g/7 oz green grapes, frozen

2 kiwis, peeled and frozen

1 banana

50 g/1¾ oz fresh spinach leaves

200 ml/7 fl oz water

juice of ½ lime

2 tbsp sliced almonds, to decorate

2 tbsp chia seeds, to decorate

100 g/3½ oz raspberries, to decorate

1. Transfer the frozen grapes, kiwi, banana and spinach leaves into a food processor and blend until smooth. Add water until a thick smoothie consistency is reached. Taste and add lime juice to your taste.

2. Heat a small frying pan over a medium heat and add the sliced almonds. Toast until just brown, about 1–2 minutes. Set aside.

3. Pour the smoothie into bowls and decorate with the almonds, chia seeds and raspberries.

PER SERVING : 349 KCALS | 12G FAT | 1.1G SAT FAT | 59.5G CARBS | 31.7G SUGAR | 16.1G FIBRE | 8.7G PROTEIN | TRACE SALT

BUCKWHEAT BREAKFAST BOWL

BUCKWHEAT HAS BEEN EATEN SINCE PALEOLITHIC TIMES. IT MAKES A TASTY CEREAL AND, BEING A SOURCE OF COMPLEX CARBOHYDRATES, PROVIDES AN EXCELLENT BOOST OF ENERGY.

20–25 mins, plus soaking and standing

None

INGREDIENTS

150 g/5½ oz buckwheat

500 ml/18 fl oz cold water

400 g/14 oz coconut yogurt

grated zest and juice of 1 orange

3 tbsp goji berries

100 g/3½ oz raspberries

1 Granny Smith apple, cored and diced

1 tbsp pumpkin seeds

2 passion fruit, pulp only

2 tsp ground cinnamon

½ tsp ground turmeric

seeds from 1 pomegranate

2 tbsp agave syrup

1. Rinse the buckwheat three times in fresh water to clean the groats. Place in a bowl with the cold water. Soak for 20 minutes. Leave to stand for 30 minutes.

2. Drain and rinse the buckwheat, and leave at room temperature – in either a sprouting tray or a sieve with a bowl beneath – for 36 hours. Rinse the buckwheat if the groats look sticky, and then once more before using.

3. Rinse, drain and divide the buckwheat between four bowls. Divide the yogurt, sprinkle over the remaining ingredients and serve.

This recipe uses buckwheat that has been sprouted for 36 hours; it can be done in less, but a longer time gives optimum nutrition.

PER SERVING : 452 KCALS | 22.4G FAT | 17.5G SAT FAT | 58G CARBS | 22.8G SUGAR | 9.8G FIBRE | 10.1G PROTEIN | 0.1G SALT

BEETROOT & POMEGRANATE SMOOTHIE BOWL

TENDER BEETROOT AND ZESTY POMEGRANATE SEEDS ARE A FABULOUS COMBINATION. THE ADDITION OF SPINACH AND WHEATGRASS MAKES THIS TASTY BREAKFAST BOWL TRULY HEALTHY.

10 mins, plus optional chilling

None

INGREDIENTS

1 large beetroot, peeled and chopped

15 g/½ oz spinach leaves

3 tbsp pomegranate seeds

100 ml/3½ fl oz water

juice of 1 orange

1 tbsp raw honey

125 g/4½ oz raw coconut yogurt (see below)

1 tsp wheatgrass powder

2 tsp buckwheat groats

2 round orange slices, halved

RAW COCONUT YOGURT

225 g/8 oz fresh or frozen coconut meat, thawed if frozen

100 ml/3½ fl oz raw coconut water

1 probiotic powder capsule

1. Pour the coconut mixture into a bowl, cover with clingfilm or foil, and leave in the kitchen overnight at warm room temperature. In the morning, you should have about 300 g/10½ oz yogurt. Remove what you need and the rest will keep in the refrigerator for up to a week.

2. Put the beetroot in a blender with the spinach, 2 tablespoons of the pomegranate seeds and half the water. Blend the contents until smooth.

3. Add the rest of the water, the orange juice, honey, 100 g/3½ oz yogurt and the wheatgrass powder to the blender. Blend again.

4. Pour the smoothie into a serving bowl and chill for an hour or so if you have time.

5. Drizzle the remaining yogurt over the smoothie. Sprinkle over the groats and decorate with the orange slices and remaining seeds.

You can try raspberries instead of pomegranate seeds for a change, or if you want to make this smoothie when pomegranates aren't in season.

PER SERVING : 604 KCALS | 32.7G FAT | 28G SAT FAT | 75.7G CARBS | 48.6G SUGAR | 17.6G FIBRE | 10.2G PROTEIN | 0.4G SALT

MATCHA
POWER SMOOTHIE

THIS IS ONE OF THE BEST GREEN SMOOTHIES YOU'LL EVER TRY – IT'S BURSTING
WITH SUPER INGREDIENTS, INCLUDING SPINACH AND AVOCADO, TO KICK-START YOUR DAY.

5 mins, plus
optional
chilling

None

④

INGREDIENTS

30 g/1 oz spinach

1 banana, peeled and chopped

1 small ripe avocado, peeled, stoned and
roughly chopped

2 kiwi fruits, peeled and chopped

125 ml/4 fl oz raw almond milk

½ tbsp raw honey

½ tsp matcha green tea powder

½ tsp wheatgrass powder

2 tsp flaked almonds

½ tsp maca powder

1. Blend the spinach, banana, avocado and one of the kiwi fruits in a blender with half the milk until you have a purée.

2. Add the honey, matcha, wheatgrass and remaining milk to the blender and blend until smooth. Pour the smoothie into your serving bowl. Chill for an hour if you have time.

3. Top your smoothie with the remaining kiwi and decorate with the flaked almonds and maca powder.

Matcha
is a Japanese
green tea rich in an
antioxidant that fights
cancers and heart disease.
The powder gives you the full
benefit of the leaves rather
than simply drinking a
brew and discarding
the leaves.

PER SERVING : 566 KCALS | 30.3G FAT | 3.3G SAT FAT | 72.1G CARBS | 37.4G SUGAR | 18.9G FIBRE | 13.2G PROTEIN | 0.1G SALT

BUBBLE & SQUEAK BREAKFAST BOWL

THIS FILLING BREAKFAST BOWL IS FULL OF GOODNESS – COLOURFUL STEAMED VEGETABLES TOSSED WITH WARMING SPICES AND TOPPED WITH A POACHED EGG AND A SPRINKLING OF NUTS.

INGREDIENTS

400 g/14 oz sweet potato, peeled and cut into chunks

200 g/7 oz kale, chopped

2 eggs

2 tsp coconut oil

1 tsp cumin seeds

1 tsp mustard seeds

1 tsp pepper

½ tsp ground turmeric

25 g/1 oz walnuts, chopped

25 g/1 oz blanched almonds, chopped

25 g/1 oz pumpkin seeds

1. Place the sweet potato in a steamer and cook for 5–6 minutes, until tender. Add the kale to the steamer for the last 2 minutes of cooking.

2. Meanwhile, bring a small saucepan of water to the boil, break the eggs into a cup, one at a time, add to the pan and poach for 4–5 minutes.

3. Heat the oil in a large frying pan or wok and add the cumin seeds, mustard seeds, pepper and turmeric. Cook until the mustard seeds begin to 'pop', then add the steamed vegetables and toss.

4. Divide the spiced vegetables between two warmed bowls and top each one with a poached egg.

5. Sprinkle each serving with walnuts, almonds and pumpkin seeds and serve immediately.

PER SERVING : 571 KCALS | 31.8G FAT | 7.9G SAT FAT | 56.7G CARBS | 11.9G SUGAR | 13.1G FIBRE | 22.7G PROTEIN | 0.5G SALT

FRUITY SWEET POTATO BREAKFAST BOWL

SWEET POTATOES ARE NOT ACTUALLY VERY SWEET IN TASTE, BUT THEY DO ADD GREAT NUTRIENTS AND A DELICIOUSLY CREAMY TEXTURE TO THIS UPLIFTINGLY COLOURFUL BREAKFAST.

1. Preheat the oven to 200°C/400°F/Gas Mark 6. Prick the sweet potatoes all over with a fork or sharp knife and bake in the preheated oven for 40–45 minutes until tender.

2. Meanwhile, dry-fry the sunflower seeds and pumpkin seeds in a frying pan until they start to pop. Transfer to a plate to cool.

INGREDIENTS

2 sweet potatoes, 175–200 g/6–7 oz each

1 tbsp sunflower seeds

1 tbsp pumpkin seeds

4 tbsp natural yogurt

1 small banana, peeled and sliced

50 g/1¾ oz blueberries

60 g/2¼ oz redcurrants

2 tsp goji berries

pinch of ground ginger

2 tbsp maple syrup

3. Place a sweet potato in each of two bowls and cut in half. Place a dollop of yogurt on each half, then add the banana, blueberries, redcurrants and goji berries and sprinkle with toasted seeds.

4. Sprinkle with ginger and drizzle with maple syrup to serve.

You can top with fruits and toasted nuts or seeds of your choice; another great combination is pineapple, mango and melon with toasted coconut flakes.

PER SERVING : 383 KCALS | 6.2G FAT | 1.3G SAT FAT | 78G CARBS | 34.6G SUGAR | 10.2G FIBRE | 7.8G PROTEIN | 0.3G SALT

WAKE-UP SALAD

WHEN YOU WANT SOMETHING SAVOURY FOR BREAKFAST, TRY THIS CRUNCHY SALAD.
IT'S LAYERED WITH DIFFERENT FRUITS AND VEGETABLES, AND IS QUICK TO PUT TOGETHER!

INGREDIENTS

125 g/4½ oz kale, chopped

1 red-skinned apple, cored and sliced

1 carrot, peeled and thinly sliced

4 Medjool dates, stoned and chopped

2 tbsp chopped raw walnuts

2 tsp sesame seeds

2 tsp hemp seeds

2 tsp sunflower seeds

DRESSING

3 tbsp cold-pressed extra virgin rapeseed oil

1 tbsp raw cider vinegar

2 tsp stone ground mustard

2 tsp maple syrup

½ tsp sea salt

½ tsp black pepper

2 spring onions, finely chopped

1. To make the dressing, combine the dressing ingredients in a lidded jar or small mixing bowl. Shake or stir well.

2. Tip the kale into a serving bowl, or two individual dishes. Add the apple and carrot, and stir in the dates and walnuts.

3. Pour the dressing over the salad and mix together. Sprinkle with the seeds to serve.

Hemp seeds are a great source of antioxidants. This recipe has unhulled seeds for a richer mineral and fibre content, but you can also use hulled seeds – both are widely available.

PER SERVING : 555 KCALS | 31.9G FAT | 2.5G SAT FAT | 66.2G CARBS | 49.6G SUGAR | 10.1G FIBRE | 8.6G PROTEIN | 1.7G SALT

SAVOURY OATMEAL WITH SALMON & AVOCADO

PORRIDGE OATS COMBINE WELL WITH SAVOURY FLAVOURS AND PROVIDE SUSTAINED ENERGY THROUGH THE MORNING. ADDING SALMON GIVES A PROTEIN AND OMEGA-3 BOOST.

INGREDIENTS

150 g/5½ oz rolled oats

350 ml/12 fl oz milk

600 ml/1 pint water

4 eggs

4 tsp creamed horseradish

200 g/7 oz hot smoked salmon, flaked

2 avocados, stoned, peeled and sliced

freshly milled black pepper (optional)

2 tbsp pumpkin seeds, toasted, to garnish

1. Place the oats in a saucepan with the milk and water. Bring to the boil and then simmer for 4–5 minutes, until thick and creamy.

2. Meanwhile, poach the eggs in a pan of simmering water for 4–5 minutes.

3. Stir the creamed horseradish and half the smoked salmon into the porridge.

4. Divide the porridge between four warmed bowls and top each one with slices of avocado, a poached egg and the remaining salmon.

5. Serve the porridge sprinkled with toasted pumpkin seeds and seasoned to taste with pepper, if using.

Sautéed mushrooms with a fried egg and a sprinkling of chives make a delicious topping variation.

PER SERVING : 547 KCALS | 32.8G FAT | 7.1G SAT FAT | 37.9G CARBS | 6G SUGAR | 9.1G FIBRE | 27.7G PROTEIN | 1.3G SALT

LIGHT LUNCHES

TOMATO, RICOTTA & GRILLED BREAD BOWL

THIS IS A DELICIOUS SUMMERY SALAD, USING ARTISAN TOMATOES, BASIL AND CREAMY RICOTTA –
A PERFECT COMBINATION. BE SURE TO BUY RIPE TOMATOES FOR AN INTENSE FLAVOUR.

INGREDIENTS

2 tbsp olive oil

1 courgette, thickly sliced

4 slices ciabatta

2 tsp balsamic vinegar

6 basil leaves, shredded

125 g/4½ oz yellow vine tomatoes,
cut into wedges

100 g/3½ oz cherry plum tomatoes, halved

1 garlic clove, peeled but left whole

¼ tsp cumin seeds

100 g/3½ oz ricotta cheese

1 tbsp pistachio nuts, chopped

1. Heat a ridged griddle pan until hot.

2. Brush 1 tablespoon of the oil over both sides of the courgette slices and the bread.

3. Place the courgettes and bread in the pan and cook for 4–5 minutes on each side, until they have chargrilled marks. Remove from the pan and set aside until needed.

4. Meanwhile, in a large bowl, whisk together the remaining oil, the vinegar and basil. Add the tomatoes and toss, then leave to stand until the courgettes are cooked.

5. Add the courgettes to the bowl and toss. Rub each slice of bread with the garlic.

6. Toast the cumin seeds in a dry frying pan for 2–3 minutes until they give off their aroma. Stir into the ricotta cheese.

7. Divide the tomato mixture between two bowls. Top with the spiced ricotta cheese and a sprinkling of the chopped nuts and serve with the toasts on the side.

PER SERVING : 640 KCALS | 33.2G FAT | 11.1G SAT FAT | 60.4G CARBS | 9.6G SUGAR | 5.9G FIBRE | 25.5G PROTEIN | 1.1G SALT

SPRING ROLL BOWL WITH SWEET GARLIC LIME SAUCE

THIS LIGHT, SUMMER DISH, DELIGHTFULLY RICH IN COLOUR, IS QUICK TO PREPARE –
THE ONLY SIGNIFICANT PREPARATION IS CUTTING UP THE VEGETABLES.

INGREDIENTS

300 g/10½ oz ready-to-wok rice noodles

1 avocado, stoned, peeled and sliced

6 cherry tomatoes, halved

¼ cucumber, halved, deseeded and sliced

4 radishes, thinly sliced

50 g/1¾ oz peanuts, chopped

2–3 fresh mint sprigs

2–3 fresh coriander sprigs

DRESSING

2 tbsp extra virgin olive oil

½ tsp sesame oil

juice and rind of ½ lime

½ tsp maple syrup

1 garlic clove, crushed

1. Place the noodles in a bowl and pour over boiling water. Leave to stand for 4 minutes, then drain.

2. To make the dressing, whisk together the olive oil, sesame oil, lime juice and rind, maple syrup and garlic.

3. Divide the noodles between two bowls and top with the avocado, tomatoes, cucumber, radishes, peanuts, mint and coriander.

4. Pour over the dressing to serve.

Always use good-quality extra virgin olive oil when making dressing, for flavour and for the nutrients it will provide. Olive oil is rich in omega 3 oils, important for brain and cell health.

PER SERVING : 650 KCALS | 41.8G FAT | 5.6G SAT FAT | 64.9G CARBS | 7.7G SUGAR | 11.1G FIBRE | 10.1G PROTEIN | 0.1G SALT

VEGETABLE RICE BOWL

THIS RECIPE INCLUDES A HOME-MADE CHILLI SAUCE – YOU CAN MAKE IT AS HOT AS YOU DARE! THE RECIPE ALSO WORKS WELL WITH PRAWNS, CHICKEN OR SHREDDED BEEF.

20 mins, plus cooling and marinating | 20 mins | 4

INGREDIENTS

1 tbsp soy sauce

1 tbsp sesame oil

1 tsp clear honey

300 g/10½ oz tofu, cut into cubes

2 tbsp sunflower oil

300 g/10½ oz basmati rice

1 large carrot, peeled and sliced into thin strings

200 g/7 oz chestnut mushrooms, sliced

55 g/2 oz mangetout, shredded

55 g/2 oz baby spinach leaves

4 eggs

1 tbsp black sesame seeds, to garnish

CHILLI SAUCE

2–3 red chillies, deseeded and finely chopped

3 garlic cloves, crushed

55 ml/2 fl oz white wine vinegar

2 tbsp caster sugar

2 tbsp sunflower oil

1. To make the chilli sauce, put the chillies, garlic cloves, the vinegar and sugar into a small pan and bring to the boil. Remove from the heat and leave to cool, then stir in 2 tablespoons of sunflower oil. Set aside.

2. Combine the soy sauce, sesame oil and honey and place in a non-metallic bowl with the tofu – leave to marinate for 10 minutes.

3. Cook the rice according to the instructions. Drain. Meanwhile, heat 1 tablespoon of the sunflower oil in a saucepan, add the carrots and mushrooms and cook for 4–5 minutes, until soft. Transfer to a plate with a slotted spoon.

4. Put the cooked rice in the pan, then add the marinated tofu, carrots, mushrooms, mangetout and spinach. Cover and cook for 2–3 minutes.

5. Meanwhile, heat the remaining sunflower oil in a frying pan, add the eggs and fry to your liking. Divide the mixture between four bowls. Top each one with a fried egg and spoonful of chilli sauce, sprinkle with the sesame seeds and serve.

PER SERVING : 698 KCALS | 20.2G FAT | 5G SAT FAT | 81.3G CARBS | 12.6G SUGAR | 4.8G FIBRE | 27.4G PROTEIN | 0.8G SALT

TOFU & SWEET POTATO BOWL

BECAUSE OF THEIR INTENSE COLOUR, THE SWEET POTATOES IN THIS REFRESHING BOWL ARE RICH IN ANTIOXIDANTS. TRY TO EAT THESE RATHER THAN WHITE POTATOES, WHICH ARE RICH IN STARCH.

15 mins, plus marinating

35–40 mins

4

INGREDIENTS

1 tbsp soy sauce

1 tbsp clear honey

1 tbsp cumin seeds

375 g/13 oz tofu, cut into chunks or strips

1 sweet potato, chopped

1 red onion, cut into wedges

2 carrots, chopped

1 tbsp olive oil

100 g/3½ oz baby spinach leaves

55 g/2 oz sugar snap peas, shredded

2 tbsp pumpkin seeds, toasted

DRESSING

85 g/3 oz hazelnuts, toasted

4 tbsp extra virgin olive oil

juice of ½ orange

juice of ½ lemon

2 tsp sherry vinegar

1. Preheat the oven to 200°C/400°F/Gas Mark 6.

2. Mix the soy sauce, honey and cumin seeds together and place the tofu in the mixture to marinate for 30 minutes.

3. Meanwhile, place the sweet potato, onion and carrots in a roasting tin, drizzle with olive oil and roast in the preheated oven for 35–40 minutes, until tender and slightly charred at the edges.

4. To make the dressing, put the hazelnuts into a food processor and process until they are finely chopped. Place in a bowl with the extra virgin olive oil, orange juice, lemon juice and vinegar and mix to combine.

5. Preheat a wok until hot, then drain the tofu, discarding the marinade. Add the tofu to the wok and stir-fry for 4–5 minutes.

6. Divide the spinach between four bowls and top with the roasted vegetables and tofu. Sprinkle over the shredded peas and the pumpkin seeds and drizzle with the dressing to serve.

PER SERVING : 537 KCALS | 40.8G FAT | 4.8G SAT FAT | 28.4G CARBS | 11.7G SUGAR | 7.8G FIBRE | 22.2G PROTEIN | 0.7G SALT

CRUNCHY NOODLE BEANFEAST

THIS BRIGHT, SUMMERY SALAD HAS DIFFERENT LAYERS OF TEXTURES AND CRUNCH TO DISCOVER AS YOU WORK THROUGH YOUR BEANFEAST BOWL!

INGREDIENTS

200 g/7 oz vermicelli rice noodles

400 g/14 oz canned butter beans, drained and rinsed

1 large carrot, peeled and cut into julienne strips

1 red chilli, deseeded and finely sliced

55 g/2 oz mangetout, shredded

¼ cucumber, cut into julienne strips

55 g/2 oz baby corn, halved lengthways

2 tbsp cashew nuts

70 g/2½ oz beansprouts

15 g/½ oz fresh mint leaves

15 g/½ oz fresh coriander leaves

15 g/½ oz fresh Thai basil leaves

2 tbsp sesame seeds, toasted

DRESSING

2 tbsp brown sugar

2 tbsp Thai fish sauce

juice of 2 limes

1 garlic clove, crushed

1. Cook the noodles according to the packet instructions. Drain and place in a bowl.

2. To make the dressing, put the sugar, fish sauce and lime juice into a jug and stir until the sugar has dissolved. Stir in the garlic.

3. Add all the remaining ingredients apart from the toasted sesame seeds to the noodles, pour in the dressing and toss together well.

4. Serve in four bowls, sprinkled with the toasted sesame seeds.

PER SERVING : 378 KCALS | 5G FAT | 0.6G SAT FAT | 69.9G CARBS | 13.1G SUGAR | 6.5G FIBRE | 12.6G PROTEIN | 2.2G SALT

COUSCOUS WITH ROAST TOMATOES & PINE NUTS

THE MEDITERRANEAN FLAVOURS OF ROASTED TOMATOES, FRESH MINT, TOASTED PINE NUTS AND FETA CHEESE COME TOGETHER IN THIS SIMPLE SUMMER DISH.

10 mins, plus 10 mins standing | 8 mins | 4

INGREDIENTS

300 g/10½ oz cherry tomatoes

3 tbsp olive oil

125 g/4½ oz couscous

200 ml/7 fl oz boiling water

30 g/1 oz pine nuts, toasted

5 tbsp fresh mint, roughly chopped

finely grated rind of 1 lemon

½ tbsp lemon juice

salt and pepper (optional)

crisp green salad, to serve (optional)

vegetarian feta cheese, to serve (optional)

1. Preheat the oven to 220°C/425°F/ Gas Mark 7. Place the tomatoes and 1 tablespoon of the oil in a ovenproof dish. Toss together, then roast for 7–8 minutes in the preheated oven until the tomatoes are soft and the skins have burst. Leave to stand for 5 minutes.

2. Put the couscous in a heatproof bowl. Pour over the boiling water, cover and leave to stand for 8–10 minutes, until soft and the liquid has been absorbed.

3. Fluff up the couscous with a fork.

4. Add the tomatoes and their juices, the pine nuts, mint, lemon rind, lemon juice and the remaining oil. Season with salt and pepper, if using, then gently toss together.

5. Serve the couscous warm or cold, with a green salad and some feta cheese, if liked.

PER SERVING : 374 KCALS | 23.2G FAT | 7.1G SAT FAT | 31.8G CARBS | 4.4G SUGAR | 4.1G FIBRE | 11.3G PROTEIN | 0.8G SALT

CHARGRILLED VEGETABLE BOWL

ROASTING VEGETABLES BRINGS OUT THEIR FLAVOUR – COOK THEM
TO JUST CHAR THE EDGES, SLIGHTLY CARAMELIZING THEM.

INGREDIENTS

1 yellow courgette, trimmed and sliced

1 green courgette, trimmed and sliced

100 g/3½ oz asparagus, trimmed and halved

1 red pepper, deseeded and chopped

1 yellow pepper, deseeded and chopped

1 red onion, cut into 8 wedges

1 fennel bulb, trimmed and sliced

4 tbsp olive oil

2 tsp cumin seeds

40 g/1¾ oz watercress

4 fresh mint sprigs

HUMMUS

200 g/7 oz canned chickpeas,
drained and rinsed

50 g/1¾ oz walnuts

2 tbsp lemon juice

2 garlic cloves, crushed

2 tbsp tahini

3–4 tbsp water

½ tsp paprika

salt and pepper (optional)

1. Preheat the oven to 200°C/400°F/Gas Mark 6.

2. Divide the chopped and sliced vegetables between two roasting tins and drizzle each one with 1 tablespoon of the oil and 1 teaspoon of the cumin seeds. Toss well to coat the vegetables with the oil. Season with salt and pepper, if using.

3. Roast the vegetables in the preheated oven for 35–40 minutes, until they start to char at the edges.

4. Meanwhile, to make the hummus, place the chickpeas and walnuts in a food processor and process until broken down.

5. With the machine running, add the lemon juice and then the garlic, tahini and remaining oil. Add 3–4 tablespoons of water to loosen and then add the paprika and salt and pepper, if using.

6. Divide the watercress and roasted vegetables between four bowls, then top with a dollop of walnut hummus. Sprinkle with mint sprigs to serve.

PER SERVING : 348 KCALS | 28.7G FAT | 3.3G SAT FAT | 21.8G CARBS | 10.2G SUGAR | 7.6G FIBRE | 7.9G PROTEIN | 0.1G SALT

VIETNAMESE SUMMER ROLL BOWL

THESE DECONSTRUCTED VIETNAMESE SUMMER ROLLS MADE WITH VEGETABLES, AROMATIC LEAVES, SUCCULENT PRAWNS AND LIGHT RICE NOODLES, ARE A PERFECT SUMMER LUNCH DISH.

INGREDIENTS

200 g/7 oz rice vermicelli noodles
20 fresh mint leaves
20 fresh coriander leaves
8 fresh Thai basil sprigs, leaves only
8 snipped fresh chives
16 large cooked tiger prawns
1 carrot, grated
½ cucumber, cut into matchsticks
2 Little Gem lettuces, leaves separated
4 tbsp salted peanuts, chopped

SAUCE

1½ tbsp caster sugar
4 tbsp lime juice
2 tbsp Thai fish sauce
2 garlic cloves, crushed
1 bird's eye chilli, finely sliced

1. Place the noodles in a large bowl and pour over boiling water. Leave to soak for 4–5 minutes, then rinse in cold water and drain.

2. Meanwhile, to make the sauce whisk together the sugar, lime juice, Thai fish sauce, garlic and chilli, until the sugar is dissolved.

3. Toss the noodles with the herbs, then divide between four bowls.

4. Top with the remaining ingredients, then pour over the sauce to serve.

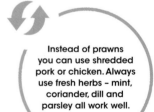

Instead of prawns you can use shredded pork or chicken. Always use fresh herbs – mint, coriander, dill and parsley all work well.

PER SERVING : 426 KCALS | 7.3G FAT | 1.4G SAT FAT | 59.2G CARBS | 9.8G SUGAR | 4.5G FIBRE | 30. 8G PROTEIN | 4.7G SALT

CUCUMBER & BUCKWHEAT YOGURT

RAW YOGURT IS A WONDERFUL BASE FOR ALL KINDS OF SAVOURY DISHES. MAKE THIS CRUNCHY AND REFRESHING YOGURT JAR FOR AN EASY LUNCH OR LIGHT BITE ON THE GO.

10 mins, plus soaking and chilling

None

4

INGREDIENTS

1 cucumber, halved, deseeded and chopped

500 g/1 lb 2 oz raw coconut yogurt (see below)

3 tbsp chopped fresh mint

1 tsp sea salt

1 tsp black pepper

100 g/3½ oz sun-dried raisins

70 g/2½ oz chopped raw walnuts

125 g/4½ oz raw buckwheat groats, soaked in water for 20 minutes, drained and rinsed

20 fresh mint leaves, to garnish

RAW COCONUT YOGURT

225 g/8 oz fresh or frozen coconut meat, thawed if frozen

100 ml/3½ fl oz raw coconut water

1 probiotic powder capsule

1. Pour the coconut mixture into a bowl, cover with clingfilm or foil, and leave in the kitchen overnight at warm room temperature. In the morning, you should have about 300 g/ 10½ oz yogurt. Remove what you need and the rest will keep in the refrigerator for up to a week.

2. Wrap the cucumber pieces in kitchen paper and squeeze to release the moisture – the kitchen paper should end up soaked.

3. Mix the yogurt, mint, salt and pepper together in a bowl.

4. Divide the ingredients evenly between four lidded jars with a 250–275 g/9 oz–9 ¾ oz capacity. Layer with the raisins, half the walnuts, the soaked groats, three quarters of the cucumber and the yogurt mixture. Garnish with the remaining cucumber and walnuts.

5. Divide the mint leaves between each of the jars and chill for 30 minutes before serving.

Try finely chopped spring onions instead of the mint and add half a teaspoon of crushed garlic to the yogurt mixture. Fresh, green, new-season's garlic is best.

PER SERVING : 659 KCALS | 45G FAT | 29.3G SAT FAT | 63.4G CARBS | 23.6G SUGAR | 15.2G FIBRE | 12G PROTEIN | 1.6G SALT

SEAWEED POWER BOWL

SEAWEED IS AN EXTRAORDINARY SOURCE OF IODINE, A NUTRIENT MISSING IN ALMOST EVERY OTHER FOOD. IODINE IS CRITICALLY IMPORTANT TO MAINTAINING A HEALTHY THYROID.

20 mins. plus standing | None | 4

INGREDIENTS

10 g/¾ oz dried kelp

½ cucumber

2 oranges

1 red chilli, deseeded and finely diced

2 carrots, grated

1 large mango, peeled, stoned and chopped

3 heads of pak choi, chopped

15 g/½ oz fresh mint leaves

15 g/½ oz fresh coriander leaves

2 tbsp salted peanuts, chopped

DRESSING

3 tbsp olive oil

grated zest and juice of 1 lime

1 tsp clear honey

1 tsp miso paste

1. Place the kelp in a bowl of water and leave to stand for 10 minutes to rehydrate.

2. Meanwhile, to make the dressing, whisk together the oil, lime zest and juice, honey and miso paste.

3. Halve the cucumber lengthways and, using a teaspoon, scoop out and discard the seeds.

4. Peel the oranges and cut them into segments.

5. Roughly chop the kelp and place in a large bowl with the cucumber, orange segments, chilli, carrot, mango, pak choi and half the mint and coriander.

6. Pour in the dressing and toss well. Divide between four bowls.

7. Sprinkle each bowl with chopped peanuts and the remaining mint and coriander.

PER SERVING : 252 KCALS | 13.4G FAT | 1.9G SAT FAT | 31G CARBS | 22.2G SUGAR | 6.4G FIBRE | 4.8G PROTEIN | 0.4G SALT

SUSHI ROLL BOWL

SUSHI IS A GREAT HEALTHY SNACK OR MEAL: THE FISH HAS OMEGA-3 FATS; RICE PROVIDES ENERGY AND PROTEIN; SEAWEED, RICH IN IODINE, IS VITAL FOR A HEALTHY THYROID. AND IT TASTES GREAT!

INGREDIENTS

300 g/10½ oz sushi rice

2 tbsp rice vinegar

1 tsp caster sugar

1 large avocado, peeled, stoned and sliced

200 g/7 oz raw tuna, sliced

200 g/7 oz raw salmon, sliced

juice of ½ lemon

4 sheets nori seaweed, shredded

¼ cucumber, cut into matchsticks

2 tbsp snipped fresh chives

1 tbsp black sesame seeds

4 tbsp gluten-free soy sauce

1. Cook the rice according to the packet instructions. When all the water has been absorbed and the rice is cooked, stir through the vinegar and sugar, then cover and leave to cool.

2. Divide the rice between four bowls.

3. Top each bowl with slices of avocado, tuna and salmon.

4. Squeeze over the lemon juice, then add the nori, cucumber, chives and sesame seeds.

5. Serve with the soy sauce.

PER SERVING : 572 KCALS | 17.7G FAT | 3.1G SAT FAT | 70.1G CARBS | 2.2G SUGAR | 7.6G FIBRE | 32G PROTEIN | 2.4G SALT

PESTO SALMON WITH SPRING VEG BOWL

SPRING VEGETABLES ARE SO TASTY THEY JUST REQUIRE GENTLE STEAMING AND A TASTY DRESSING. THIS LEMON DRESSING CUTS THROUGH THE RICHNESS OF THE PESTO SALMON PERFECTLY.

INGREDIENTS

200 g/7 oz fresh or frozen peas

200 g/7 oz fresh broad beans

200 g/7 oz asparagus, woody stems discarded

200 g/7 oz baby carrots, scrubbed

4 skinless salmon fillets, each weighing 150 g/5½ oz

4 tbsp pesto

2 tbsp sunflower seeds, toasted

2 tbsp pumpkin seeds, toasted

2 tbsp shredded fresh basil

LEMON DRESSING

4 tbsp extra virgin olive oil

grated rind and juice of 1 lemon

1. Place all the vegetables in a steamer and cook for 10–12 minutes, until tender.

2. Meanwhile, preheat the grill to hot and line a baking sheet with foil. Place the salmon on the prepared baking sheet and spoon over the pesto. Cook under the grill for 3–4 minutes on each side.

3. Mix the oil with the lemon rind and juice to make the lemon dressing, and toss with the cooked vegetables.

4. Divide the vegetables between four warmed shallow bowls and top each one with a salmon fillet.

5. Sprinkle with the sunflower seeds, pumpkin seeds and shredded basil and serve.

PER SERVING : 646 KCALS | 42.9G FAT | 7.6G SAT FAT | 21.9G CARBS | 7.7G SUGAR | 9.7G FIBRE | 42G PROTEIN | 0.7G SALT

TUNA POKE BOWL

A POKE BOWL IS A STAPLE HAWAIIAN DISH THAT NORMALLY CONTAINS RAW FISH AND ALL SORTS OF VIBRANT INGREDIENTS. THIS ONE INCLUDES TUNA AND WAKAME.

15 mins, plus soaking

25 mins

4

INGREDIENTS

200 g/7 oz brown rice

15 g/½ oz wakame, soaked in lukewarm water for 10–15 minutes and roughly chopped

2 tbsp gluten-free soy sauce

2 tbsp rice wine vinegar

225 g/8 oz good-quality raw tuna, sliced

1 avocado, stoned, peeled and sliced

8 cherry tomatoes, halved

4 spring onions, thinly sliced

½ tsp chilli flakes

2 tbsp olive oil

1 tbsp black sesame seeds

1. Cook the rice according to the packet instructions.

2. Place the cooked rice in a bowl and stir in half the soaked wakame, half the soy sauce and the rice wine vinegar. Divide between four bowls and top with the tuna, avocado, tomatoes and spring onions.

3. Mix the remaining soy sauce and wakame with the chilli flakes, olive oil and sesame seeds in a small bowl. Sprinkle over the poke bowls to serve.

If you don't want to eat your fish raw, flash-fry it quickly in a pan before adding to your dish.

PER SERVING : 399 KCALS | 15.4G FAT | 2.2G SAT FAT | 45.5G CARBS | 2.4G SUGAR | 5.3G FIBRE | 20.4G PROTEIN | 1.3G SALT

SPICY CHICKEN NOODLE SOUP

THIS QUICK, WHOLESOME SOUP IS A WINNER FOR AN INSTANT MEAL THAT'S PACKED WITH GOODNESS. THE MAIN FLAVOUR COMES FROM MISO, A HIGHLY NUTRITIOUS FERMENTED PASTE.

INGREDIENTS

300 ml/10 fl oz chicken stock

18 g/¾ oz miso paste

2-cm/¾-inch piece fresh ginger, peeled and finely grated

1 red chilli, deseeded and thinly sliced

1 carrot, cut into thin strips

200 g/7 oz pak choi, roughly chopped

150 g/5½ oz dried egg thread noodles, cooked

1 cooked chicken breast, shredded

dash of dark soy sauce

4 spring onions, trimmed and finely chopped

1. Place the stock together with 250 ml/9 fl oz boiling water in a saucepan and bring to the boil over a medium–high heat. Add the miso paste and simmer for 1–2 minutes.

2. Add the ginger, chilli, carrot, pak choi, cooked noodles and chicken. Simmer for a further 4–5 minutes. Season to taste with soy sauce.

3. Scatter the spring onions in the base of two serving dishes and pour the soup over. Serve immediately.

PER SERVING : 511 KCALS | 7.9G FAT | 2.3G SAT FAT | 66.4G CARBS | 7G SUGAR | 7.1G FIBRE | 41.3G PROTEIN | 2.5G SALT

KOREAN BULGOGI BOWL

THIS KOREAN BULGOGI RECIPE HAS LEAN HIGH-PROTEIN STEAK, BROWN RICE THAT LEAVES YOU FEELING FULLER FOR LONGER AND VITAMIN-PACKED FRUIT AND VEG. IT'S ALSO A TASTE SENSATION.

15 mins plus marinating

30 mins

4

INGREDIENTS

500 g/1lb 2oz bavette or skirt steak, fat trimmed off and thinly sliced

225 g/8 oz long grain brown rice

4 tsp sesame seeds

200 g/7 oz tenderstem broccoli, stems cut into thick slices and florets halved lengthways

1–2 tbsp sunflower oil

MARINADE

2 tbsp reduced-salt soy sauce

2 tbsp rice wine vinegar

4 tsp molasses sugar

2 tsp gochujang Korean chilli paste or other red chilli paste

2 garlic cloves, finely chopped

5 cm/2 inch piece root ginger, peeled and coarsely grated

1 apple, unpeeled, coarsely grated

TO SERVE

175 g/6oz carrot, coarsely grated

115 g/4 oz red cabbage, thinly shredded

½ small mango, diced

6 tbsp kimchi

1 tbsp fresh coriander sprigs, torn

1. To make the marinade, add the soy sauce, vinegar and sugar to a medium-sized shallow china or glass bowl. Mix in the gochujang chilli paste, garlic, ginger and apple to form a smooth paste. Add the steak slices and toss together. Cover the bowl with clingfilm and marinate in the refrigerator for at least ½–1 hour.

2. When almost ready to serve, add the rice to a saucepan of boiling water, bring the water back to the boil then simmer for about 30 minutes until tender. Toast the sesame seeds in a dry pan for 2–3 minutes until just beginning to colour then take the pan off the heat.

3. Add the broccoli florets and stems to a wok or large frying pan with 2 tbsp cold water. Cover and cook for 2 minutes then drain off the water, add 1 tablespoon of the oil and stir fry the broccoli over a high heat for 1 minute. Scoop out of the pan and reserve.

4. Heat the remaining oil in the pan, drain the steak, reserving the marinade then gradually add the steak slices to the hot wok until they are all in the pan and stir fry over a high heat for 2–3 minutes until browned.

5. Pour in the remaining marinade and 2 tbsp cold water then cook for 1–2 minutes to make a sauce.

6. Drain and spoon the hot just-cooked rice into four large serving bowls, top with the steak and broccoli and sprinkle with the toasted sesame seeds. Add little piles of the grated carrot, shredded cabbage, diced mango and kimchi to the bowls, then sprinkle with coriander. Serve immediately.

PER SERVING : 667 KCALS | 24.5G FAT | 6.9G SAT FAT | 70G CARBS | 18G SUGAR | 7.3G FIBRE | 41.7G PROTEIN | 1.4G SALT

CHICKEN & CHICKPEA POWER BOWL

CHICKEN AND CHICKPEAS ARE BOTH RICH IN PROTEIN, SO THIS RECIPE GIVES YOU A DOUBLE BOOST! WITH A LOVELY PEANUTTY DRESSING, THIS ONE IS HARD TO RESIST.

INGREDIENTS

400 g/14 oz canned chickpeas, drained and rinsed

400 g/14 oz butternut squash, peeled, deseeded and chopped into bite-sized pieces

2 red peppers, deseeded and chopped

1 red onion, roughly chopped

3 tbsp olive oil

½ tsp paprika

½ tsp cumin seeds

2 large chicken breasts

50 g/1¾ oz fresh watercress, to serve

SAUCE

½ tsp groundnut oil

1 garlic clove, crushed

½ tsp chilli flakes

½ tbsp soft light brown sugar

1 tsp gluten-free soy sauce

2 tbsp smooth peanut butter

300 ml/10 fl oz coconut milk

1. Preheat the oven to 200°C/400°F/Gas Mark 6.

2. Place the chickpeas, squash, red peppers and onion in two roasting tins, add 1 tablespoon of olive oil to each tin and toss to coat the vegetables. Roast in the preheated oven for 30–35 minutes, until the vegetables are tender and the edges charred.

3. Meanwhile, mix the remaining olive oil with the paprika and cumin seeds.

4. Place the chicken between two sheets of greaseproof paper and flatten slightly with a rolling pin or mallet (this helps them to cook more evenly).

5. Rub the chicken with the spiced oil. Preheat a griddle pan to hot.

6. Add the chicken to the pan and cook for 4–5 minutes each side, until cooked through. Leave to rest for 1–2 minutes, then cut into strips.

7. Meanwhile, to make the sauce heat the groundnut oil in a saucepan, add the garlic and chilli flakes and cook for 30 seconds, then add the sugar and cook for 1 minute. Stir in the soy sauce and peanut butter, then add the coconut milk, a little at a time, stirring constantly, until the sauce has the consistency you want.

8. Serve the roasted vegetables and chickpeas on a bed of watercress in four bowls, topped with strips of chicken and the sauce.

PER SERVING : 450 KCALS | 20.8G FAT | 3.9G SAT FAT | 35G CARBS | 13G SUGAR | 8.1G FIBRE | 30.6G PROTEIN | 0.4G SALT

SALADS

COLOURFUL COLESLAW

THIS COLESLAW IS FULL OF NUTRIENTS – FIBRE, ANTIOXIDANTS AND ESSENTIAL FATS. FOR A BALANCED MEAL, SERVE WITH GRILLED FISH OR BARBECUED CHICKEN.

1. To make the dressing, put the yogurt, mustard, lime juice, honey and tahini into a large bowl and mix to combine.

2. Add the remaining ingredients and toss well to coat with the dressing.

INGREDIENTS

100 g/3½ oz red cabbage, shredded

100 g/3½ oz white cabbage, shredded

2 carrots, grated

1 small red onion, thinly sliced

1 red pepper, deseeded and thinly sliced

1 yellow pepper, deseeded and thinly sliced

1 fennel bulb, trimmed and shredded

4 radishes, thinly sliced

1 tbsp chopped fresh basil

1 tbsp chopped fresh parsley

1 tbsp chopped fresh mint

3 tbsp pine nuts, toasted

2 tbsp hemp seeds, toasted

DRESSING

4 tbsp natural yogurt

½ tsp Dijon mustard

juice of 1 lime

½ tsp honey

2 tsp tahini

For a balanced meal, serve this coleslaw with broiled fish, such as tuna or mackerel fillets. Or if you are having a summer barbecue, try it with barbecued chicken or chops.

PER SERVING : 174 CALS | 9.2G FAT | 1.1G SAT FAT | 19.4G CARBS | 10.2G SUGAR | 6G FIBRE | 6.1G PROTEIN | 0.2G SALT

SWEETCORN RICE & BEAN BOWL

THIS ATTRACTIVE SALAD CAN BE SERVED WARM OR COLD. MIXING RICE AND BEANS ENSURES A COMPLETE BALANCE OF PROTEIN FOR THE MEAL – PERFECT FOR VEGETARIANS.

INGREDIENTS

100 g/3½ oz brown basmati rice

100 g/3½ oz wild rice

400 g/14 oz canned mixed beans, drained and rinsed

200 g/7 oz frozen sweetcorn, thawed

100 g/3½ oz frozen peas, thawed

1 small red onion, finely sliced

55 g/2 oz pistachio nuts, chopped

1 large carrot, peeled and grated

1 large avocado, sliced

15 g/½ oz fresh coriander leaves, to serve

salt and pepper (optional)

DRESSING

juice and zest of 1 lime

2 tbsp extra virgin olive oil

1 tsp honey

1 red chilli, deseeded and diced

15 g/½ oz fresh mint leaves, chopped

1. Cook the rice according to the packet instructions.

2. Meanwhile, to make the dressing, whisk together the lime zest and juice, oil, honey, chilli and mint.

3. Drain the rice, place it in a large bowl and mix in the beans, sweetcorn, peas, onion, nuts and carrot. Stir in the dressing and season to taste with salt and pepper, if using.

4. Divide between four bowls, top with the avocado slices and sprinkle with coriander leaves to serve.

So many things can be added to this bowl – choose your favourite beans, nuts and vegetables. You could also add fruit – try chopped apricots or blueberries for added colour.

PER SERVING : 579 CALS | 24.4G FAT | 3.4G SAT FAT | 77.9G CARBS | 9.6G SUGAR | 14.9G FIBRE | 16.6G PROTEIN | 0.1G SALT

LENTIL, GRAPE & FETA SALAD

THIS IS A FABULOUS COMBINATION – CREAMY FETA CHEESE WITH CRUNCHY NUTS AND SWEET GRAPES, TOPPED WITH A CITRUS AND HERB DRESSING.

INGREDIENTS

1 cos lettuce

25 g/1 oz rocket leaves

55 g/2 oz seedless red grapes

55 g/2 oz seedless white grapes

300 g/10½ oz cooked Puy lentils

4 spring onions, trimmed and sliced

1 red pepper, deseeded and thinly sliced

70 g/2½ oz pecan nuts

125 g/4½ oz feta cheese, crumbled

DRESSING

3 tbsp extra virgin olive oil

1 tsp walnut oil

1 tsp raspberry vinegar

juice of ½ lemon

2 tsp maple syrup

1 tsp wholegrain mustard

½ garlic clove, crushed

2 tsp chopped fresh mint

2 tsp chopped fresh parsley

salt and pepper (optional)

1. To make the dressing, whisk together the olive oil, walnut oil, vinegar, lemon juice, maple syrup, mustard, garlic, mint and parsley. Season to taste with salt and pepper, if using.

2. Divide the lettuce and rocket between four large shallow bowls.

3. Halve the red grapes and the white grapes. Mix the lentils, spring onions, red grapes, white grapes and red pepper together and spoon the mixture over the lettuce and rocket.

4. Chop the pecan nuts. Then sprinkle the nuts and cheese over the salad, drizzle with the dressing and serve immediately.

Make double or treble the quantity of dressing, then you can store the remainder in a jar or bottle in the fridge.

PER SERVING : 475 CALS | 32.8G FAT | 7.5G SAT FAT | 35.1G CARBS | 13.4G SUGAR | 12.5G FIBRE | 16G PROTEIN | 0.8G SALT

SUMMER ABUNDANCE SALAD

THIS RECIPE INCLUDES VEGETABLES, FRUIT AND PULSES TO GIVE A BALANCED MEAL IN A BOWL, TOPPED WITH A DELICIOUS LEMON DRESSING TO BRING IT ALL TO LIFE.

INGREDIENTS

1 tbsp sesame seeds

2 tbsp pecan nuts, roughly chopped

35 g/1¼ oz rocket leaves

1 large carrot, peeled

100 g/3½ oz cooked beetroot, sliced

1 dessert apple, cored and sliced

400 g/14 oz canned chickpeas, drained

2 celery sticks, sliced

50 g/1¾ oz blackberries

10 g/¼ oz alfalfa sprouts

DRESSING

3 tbsp extra virgin olive oil

1 tbsp lemon juice

grated zest of ½ lemon

½ tsp Dijon mustard

½ tsp clear honey

salt and pepper (optional)

1. Toast the seeds and nuts in a dry frying pan until lightly golden.

2. To make the dressing, whisk together the oil, lemon juice, lemon zest, mustard and honey in a bowl. Season to taste with salt and pepper, if using.

3. Divide the rocket, carrot, beetroot, apple, chickpeas, celery, blackberries and alfalfa sprouts between four bowls, then drizzle with the dressing and serve.

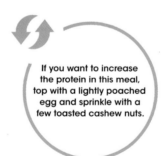

If you want to increase the protein in this meal, top with a lightly poached egg and sprinkle with a few toasted cashew nuts.

PER SERVING : 270 KCALS | 16.3G FAT | 1.9G SAT FAT | 24.8G CARBS | 12.1G SUGAR | 7.6G FIBRE | 6.6G PROTEIN | 0.2G SALT

JEWEL SALAD WITH RANCH DRESSING

A BEAUTIFUL SALAD IS ALWAYS A WELCOME ADDITION TO THE DINNER TABLE. THIS VIBRANT DISH IS COMPLEMENTED BY A PROTEIN-RICH VARIATION OF THE CLASSIC AMERICAN RANCH DRESSING.

20 mins, plus soaking | None | 4

INGREDIENTS

2 large tomatoes, deseeded

1 cucumber

½ red onion

1 carrot

1 yellow pepper, deseeded

10 red radishes

8 tbsp mixed chopped soft herbs, such as parsley, mint and coriander

zest and juice of ½ lemon

4 tbsp cold-pressed extra virgin olive oil

½ tsp sea salt

½ tsp black pepper

RANCH DRESSING

100 g/3½ oz raw cashew nuts, soaked in water for 2 hours, drained and rinsed

1 tbsp raw cider vinegar

125 ml/4 fl oz raw coconut milk

1 garlic clove, crushed

½ tsp sea salt

2 spring onions, finely chopped

2 tbsp chopped fresh parsley

1. To make the dressing, put the soaked nuts, vinegar, 60 ml/2 fl oz coconut milk, the garlic and salt in a blender. Blend until you have a smooth paste. Add the rest of the coconut milk a little at a time until you have a fairly thick mix. It should be a cross between a dip and a pouring consistency. Stir in the spring onions and parsley.

2. To make the salad, finely chop the vegetables and put them in a large serving bowl, or smaller individual ones. Stir in all the remaining salad ingredients and serve.

You can vary the salad ingredients according to what you have, or what is in season. For example, try swapping the yellow pepper for sweetcorn kernels.

PER SERVING : 360 CALS | 28.8G FAT | 7.2G SAT FAT | 22.7G CARBS | 9.4G SUGAR | 6G FIBRE | 7.5G PROTEIN | 1.5G SALT

SEAWEED & SESAME SALAD

SEAWEED IS A FANTASTIC SOURCE OF MINERALS AND FIBRE – AND IF YOU CAN FIND A BAG OF MIXED SEAWEED, THE VARIETY OF COLOURS AND TEXTURES IS BEAUTIFUL TO LOOK AT.

5 mins, plus soaking

None

INGREDIENTS

1 x 20g/¾ oz pack of mixed dried seaweed, soaked in water for 5–10 minutes

1 large spring onion, finely chopped

1 red radish, finely chopped

2 tsp sesame seeds, to garnish

DRESSING

1 tbsp cold-pressed extra virgin sesame oil

1 tbsp raw rice vinegar

1 tbsp raw coconut aminos

1 tsp chopped red chilli

2 tsp mirin

1 tsp organic miso paste

1. While the seaweed is soaking, make the dressing. Add the sesame oil, rice vinegar, coconut aminos, chilli, mirin and miso paste to a small bowl and stir vigorously, to combine.

2. Once the seaweed is tender and reconstituted, drain it thoroughly in a colander and rinse.

3. Divide the seaweed between two shallow bowls and drizzle the dressing over it, tossing lightly.

4. Sprinkle the onion and radish over the salad and garnish with the sesame seeds to serve.

Dried seaweed mixes are widely available in health-food shops and online. Some kinds you can try are wakame, dulse, agar agar, miyoek, chondrus, gigartina and kelp.

PER SERVING : 137 CALS | 9.2G FAT | 1.4G SAT FAT | 8.2G CARBS | 2.5G SUGAR | 1.1G FIBRE | 11.6G PROTEIN | 0.5G SALT

CAULIFLOWER SALAD WITH APPLE & NUTS

RAW CAULIFLOWER, WITH ITS MILD, SLIGHTLY NUTTY FLAVOUR, TASTES WONDERFUL MIXED WITH CRISP SPIRALS OF APPLE, A SCATTERING OF WALNUTS AND A FABULOUS TANGY DRESSING.

15 mins | None | 4

INGREDIENTS

1 cauliflower, divided into small florets

1 large red-skinned dessert apple, cored and chopped

2 tbsp sunflower seeds

1 tbsp sesame seeds

3 tbsp chopped raw walnuts

1 large sweet potato, peeled and spiralized

1 small red onion, spiralized

1 tbsp cold-pressed extra virgin rapeseed oil

½ tsp sea salt

¼ tsp black pepper

2 tsp chopped fresh dill, to garnish

DRESSING

3 tbsp raw coconut yogurt

juice of ½ lemon

2 tsp grated fresh horseradish

1 tbsp chopped fresh dill

1 garlic clove, crushed

½ tsp sea salt

½ tsp black pepper

1. Put the cauliflower florets in a large bowl. Add three quarters of the apple, all of the seeds and 2 tablespoons of the walnuts.

2. Beat all the dressing ingredients together in a small bowl and pour over the cauliflower mix. Stir well until everything is coated.

3. Divide the sweet potato spirals between four serving dishes and sprinkle the onion spirals on top. Drizzle over the rapeseed oil, then add the salt and pepper.

4. Spoon the cauliflower mixture into the serving dishes. Top with the remaining apple and walnuts, and garnish with the dill to serve.

PER SERVING : 263 CALS | 14.2G FAT | 3.6G SAT FAT | 30.8G CARBS | 12.4G SUGAR | 7.5G FIBRE | 7.1G PROTEIN | 1.7G SALT

RAINBOW SALAD

MANGO, PEPPERS, BLUEBERRIES AND TOMATOES ARE ALL RICH IN ANTIOXIDANTS, AND NUTS AND SEEDS PROVIDE THE ESSENTIAL FATS NEEDED FOR HEALTHY CELL MEMBRANES.

INGREDIENTS

200 g/7 oz halloumi cheese

40 g/1½ oz rocket

1 mango, peeled, stoned and chopped

12 cherry tomatoes, halved

1 yellow pepper, deseeded and sliced

35 g/1¼ oz mangetout, shredded

4 spring onions, thinly sliced

50 g/1¾ oz blueberries

35 g/1¼ oz sunflower seeds, toasted

35 g/1¼ oz pumpkin seeds, toasted

25 g/1 oz alfalfa sprouts

DRESSING

3 tbsp olive oil

juice of 1 lemon

1 tsp honey

1 tsp mustard

1. To make the dressing, whisk together the oil, lemon juice, honey and mustard.

2. Add the cheese to a dry frying pan and cook for 3–4 minutes on each side, until golden.

3. Meanwhile, divide the rocket between four bowls, then top with the mango, tomatoes, yellow pepper, mangetout, spring onions and blueberries.

4. Top each serving with slices of cheese and sprinkle with the sunflower and pumpkin seeds and alfalfa sprouts.

5. Drizzle over the dressing and serve immediately.

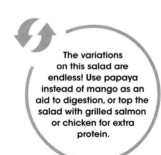

The variations on this salad are endless! Use papaya instead of mango as an aid to digestion, or top the salad with grilled salmon or chicken for extra protein.

PER SERVING : 438 CALS | 32.9G FAT | 10.9G SAT FAT | 23.4G CARBS | 16.6G SUGAR | 4.8G FIBRE | 17G PROTEIN | 1.5G SALT

AVOCADO HERO SALAD

THIS SALAD IS FULL OF GORGEOUS TEXTURES, JUXTAPOSING CREAMY AVOCADO WITH CRUNCHY ASPARAGUS TIPS, AND IS RICH IN MONOUNSATURATED FATS, SOLUBLE FIBRE AND VITAMIN E.

10 mins, plus sprouting

None

INGREDIENTS

85 g/3 oz dry green peas
suitable for sprouting

85 g/3 oz whole quinoa seeds
suitable for sprouting

70 g/2½ oz baby spinach

70 g/2½ oz baby asparagus tips

16 baby plum tomatoes

30 g/1 oz fresh watercress

2 ripe avocados, stoned, peeled and
sliced into bite-sized pieces

2 tbsp raw pine nuts

8 fresh basil sprigs

½ tbsp cold-pressed extra virgin olive oil

DRESSING

2 tbsp cold-pressed extra virgin olive oil

½ tbsp raw wine vinegar

2 tsp raw honey

1 tsp stoneground mustard

½ tsp sea salt

½ tsp pepper

1. To sprout the peas, put them in a wide-necked glass jar and soak them overnight in tepid water, covered with muslin or a similar material. In the morning, drain and rinse the peas and fill the jar with fresh water. Drain and rinse the peas twice a day for 5 days, until they have sprouted. Rinse and drain to use.

2. To sprout the quinoa, use the same method as the peas but soak them for only 4 hours. They will sprout in about 2 days.

3. Arrange the spinach, all but four of the asparagus tips and the plum tomatoes in two serving dishes with most of the watercress.

4. Arrange three quarters of the avocado slices in the dishes with the remaining watercress and the sprouted peas and quinoa. Sprinkle three quarters of the pine nuts on top.

5. In a small bowl, mash the remaining avocado with the remaining pine nuts, six of the basil sprigs and the half-tablespoon of olive oil until you have a rough purée.

6. Make the dressing by thoroughly combining the ingredients in a small dish. Spoon most of this over the salad.

7. Finish the salad by arranging two asparagus tips in the centre of each dish, followed by half the avocado purée and a basil sprig. Drizzle over the rest of the dressing to serve.

PER SERVING : 813 CALS | 48.5G FAT | 6.2G SAT FAT | 80.6G CARBS | 13.3G SUGAR | 27.1G FIBRE | 23.4G PROTEIN | 1.6G SALT

GADO GADO SALAD

TOSSING CAULIFLOWER AND BROCCOLI WITH BEANSPROUTS AND CUCUMBER AND ADDING A TOASTED PEANUT AND SOY DRESSING TURNS EVERYDAY INGREDIENTS INTO SOMETHING EXOTIC.

INGREDIENTS

250 g/9 oz cauliflower, cored and cut into small florets

115 g/4 oz broccoli, destalked and cut into small florets

115 g/4 oz Savoy cabbage, shredded

150 g/5½ oz ready-to-eat beansprouts

300 g/10½ oz cucumber, peeled, halved lengthways, deseeded and thickly sliced

1 red pepper, halved, deseeded and finely chopped

DRESSING

2 tbsp groundnut oil

85 g/3 oz unsalted peanuts, finely chopped

2 garlic cloves, finely chopped

2 tbsp gluten-free soy sauce

juice of 2 limes

½ red chilli, deseeded and finely chopped

1. Put the cauliflower, broccoli, cabbage, beansprouts, cucumber and red pepper in a salad bowl and toss gently together.

2. To make the dressing, heat 1 tablespoon of the oil in a frying pan over a medium heat. Add the peanuts and garlic and stir-fry for 2—3 minutes, or until lightly browned. Remove from the heat and stir in the soy sauce, lime juice, chilli and remaining oil, then leave to cool.

3. When ready to eat, spoon the dressing over the salad and toss gently together. Spoon into four bowls, then serve immediately.

 Popular in Chinese and Asian recipes, mung beansprouts are widely available in supermarkets all year round. Low in calories, they can be added to salads in place of noodles or rice.

PER SERVING : 259 CALS | 17.8G FAT | 2.6G SAT FAT | 20.4G CARBS | 8.2G SUGAR | 6.6G FIBRE | 10.8G PROTEIN | 1.2G SALT

CUCUMBER NOODLE BOWL WITH THAI DRESSING

THIS SPICY THAI SALAD IS FULL OF CHOLESTEROL-LOWERING FOODS, SUCH AS BEETROOT, KALE AND SEAWEED. IT ALSO FEATURES A YUMMY PEANUT TOPPING FOR A HEALTHY HEART.

INGREDIENTS

1 beetroot, peeled and spiralized

½ cucumber, spiralized

70 g/2½ oz kale, chopped

½ red onion, thinly sliced

1 small carrot, peeled and thinly sliced

40 g/1½ oz raw peanuts

2 tsp ground red seaweed

20 g/¾ oz fresh coconut flakes, to garnish

1 tbsp fresh coriander leaves, to garnish

DRESSING

2 tbsp cold-pressed extra virgin sesame oil

2 tsp organic miso paste

juice of ½ lime

1-cm/½-inch piece of fresh ginger, minced

1 large garlic clove, minced

1 small red chilli, minced

2 tsp raw peanut butter

salt (optional)

1. Arrange all but a few strands of the beetroot in two serving bowls. Add all of the cucumber strands.

2. Add the kale to the bowls and top with the onion and carrot.

3. To make the dressing, combine all the ingredients in a small bowl and mix well. Spoon this over the beetroot salad.

4. Run the peanuts under cold water, then pat them dry so they are just slightly damp. On a plate, roll them in the seaweed until they are thoroughly coated and sprinkle over the salad.

5. Add the coconut flakes and coriander leaves to the salad. Garnish with the remaining beetroot strands to serve.

You can use raw almond butter or raw cashew butter in the dressing and you can choose either of these nuts for the garnish.

PER SERVING : 409 CALS | 30.4G FAT | 6.7G SAT FAT | 29.1G CARBS | 12.1G SUGAR | 8.4G FIBRE | 11.5G PROTEIN | 0.7G SALT

SALMON & SOYA BEAN SALAD

SALMON IS A REAL SUPERFOOD – NOT ONLY DELICIOUS, BUT RICH IN PROTEIN
AND OMEGA-3 FATS, WHICH ARE HUGELY IMPORTANT FOR PHYSICAL AND MENTAL HEALTH.

15 mins

6–8 mins

4

INGREDIENTS

400 g/14 oz salmon fillets

200 g/7 oz frozen soya beans, thawed

200 g/7 oz frozen peas, thawed

100 g/3½ oz roasted red pepper,
cut into strips

40 g/1½ oz fresh rocket

15 g/½ oz fresh dill, chopped

pepper (optional)

DRESSING

3 tbsp olive oil

1½ tbsp lemon juice

1 tsp wholegrain mustard

1 tsp honey

1. For the dressing, whisk the olive oil, lemon juice, mustard and honey together in a small bowl. Set aside.

2. Grill the salmon fillets under a medium heat for 3–4 minutes on each side, until the fish is opaque and flaky when separated with a fork. Break into large flakes.

3. Meanwhile bring a large saucepan of water to the boil and tip the soya beans and peas into the water. Cook for 3–4 minutes, until just tender. Drain and run under cold water to refresh.

4. Place the salmon flakes, beans, peas, pepper strips, rocket and dill in a large bowl. Pour over the dressing and season to taste with pepper, if using. Toss well to combine. Divide between four bowls and serve.

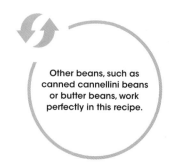

Other beans, such as canned cannellini beans or butter beans, work perfectly in this recipe.

PER SERVING : 446 CALS | 30.3G FAT | 5.2G SAT FAT | 13G CARBS | 5.8G SUGAR | 5.1G FIBRE | 29.9G PROTEIN | 0.3G SALT

HARISSA CHICKEN SALAD

CAPTURE THE FLAVOURS OF MOROCCO WITH THIS SPICY BROWN RICE SALAD FLECKED WITH DICED DRIED APRICOTS AND GLISTENING RAISINS, AND TOSSED WITH GREEN KALE.

INGREDIENTS

250 g/9 oz easy-cook brown rice

2 tsp tomato purée

500 g/1 lb 2 oz skinless chicken breast fillets

85 g/3 oz ready-to-eat dried apricots, diced

55 g/2 oz raisins

55 g/2 oz pickled lemons, drained and finely chopped

1 small red onion, finely chopped

85 g/3 oz kale, shredded

3 tbsp pine nuts, toasted

DRESSING

2 tsp harissa

4 tbsp olive oil

juice of 1 lemon

salt and pepper (optional)

1. Put the rice in a saucepan of boiling water. Bring back to the boil, then simmer for 25–30 minutes, or until tender. Drain, then transfer to a salad bowl.

2. Put the harissa, oil and lemon juice in a jam jar, season with salt and pepper, if using, screw on the lid and shake well.

3. Spoon 2 tablespoons of the dressing into a bowl and mix in the tomato purée. Preheat the grill to high and line the grill pan with foil. Put the chicken on the foil. Brush some of the tomato dressing over the chicken, then grill for 15–18 minutes, turning the meat and brushing it with the remaining tomato dressing halfway through. Cut through a breast to check that the meat is no longer pink and any juices run clear. Cover and leave to cool.

4. Drizzle the rest of the dressing over the rice. Add the apricots, raisins, lemon and onion, then toss together and leave to cool.

5. Add the kale and pine nuts to the salad and stir well. Thinly slice the chicken, arrange it over the salad and serve.

PER SERVING : 668 CALS | 24G FAT | 3.1G SAT FAT | 78.8G CARBS | 22.1G SUGAR | 6.4G FIBRE | 36.3G PROTEIN | 0.9G SALT

GRILLED CHICKEN & SLAW BOWL

HERE'S A PERFECT MID-WEEK MEAL FOR ESSENTIAL PROTEIN AND ENERGY: CRUNCHY VEGETABLES DRIZZLED IN A SPICY MAYONNAISE AND TOPPED WITH TENDER SLICES OF CHICKEN.

INGREDIENTS

4 x 150 g/5½ oz boneless, skinless chicken breasts

1 tsp smoked paprika

salt and pepper (optional)

12 fresh rocket leaves, to garnish

COLESLAW

2 carrots, peeled and grated

1 fennel bulb, trimmed and thinly sliced

1 beetroot, grated

150 g/5½ oz red cabbage, shredded

150 g/5½ oz white cabbage, shredded

4 radishes, thinly sliced

1 red onion, peeled and thinly sliced

15 g/½ oz fresh mixed herbs, such as parsley, dill, mint and coriander, chopped

juice of 1 lemon

2 tbsp extra virgin olive oil

250 g/9 oz natural yogurt

1 tbsp gluten-free wholegrain mustard

1. To make the coleslaw, place all the coleslaw ingredients together in a large bowl. Toss together really well and set aside.

2. Preheat the grill to a medium heat. Place the chicken breasts between two sheets of greaseproof paper and flatten with a rolling pin or mallet, to a thickness of 1–2 cm/ ½–¾ inch.

3. Season the chicken with paprika, and salt and pepper, if using. Grill for 4–5 minutes on each side, until the chicken is tender and the juices run clear when a skewer is inserted into the thickest part of the meat.

4. Divide the coleslaw between four bowls and top with slices of chicken breast and the rocket leaves.

Flattening the chicken breasts helps them to cook more quickly and evenly. Remove the skin as this is where the fat is.

PER SERVING : 362 CALS | 13.4G FAT | 3.1G SAT FAT | 21.9G CARBS | 12.7G SUGAR | 6.1G FIBRE | 39.2G PROTEIN | 0.5G SALT

TURKEY WALDORF BOWL

THIS TURKEY SALAD, PAIRED WITH LOTS OF CRUNCHY RAW FRUIT
AND VEGETABLES AND TAHINI AND LIME DRESSING, IS HARD TO BEAT.

20 mins | None | 4

INGREDIENTS

350 g/12 oz cooked turkey, shredded

2 celery sticks, thinly sliced

50 g/1¾ oz red cabbage, shredded

2 crisp apples, cored and chopped

100 g/3½ oz seedless red grapes, halved

100 g/3½ oz Chinese cabbage, shredded

75 g/2¾ ounces walnuts, toasted

50 g/1¾ oz pecan nuts, toasted

DRESSING

3 tbsp gluten-free tahini

2 tbsp lime juice

2 tsp agave syrup

1 tsp soy sauce

salt and pepper (optional)

1. Whisk together the tahini, lime juice, agave syrup and soy sauce and season to taste with salt and pepper, if using.

2. Lightly toss together the remaining ingredients, then toss again with the dressing. Divide between four large shallow bowls and serve immediately.

You can use chicken or even smoked mackerel in place of turkey in this salad. If using mackerel, add a little creamed horseradish to the dressing for a real kick.

PER SERVING : 482 CALS | 29.3G FAT | 3.4G SAT FAT | 29.1G CARBS | 17.4G SUGAR | 6.8G FIBRE | 32.8G PROTEIN | 0.5G SALT

MAIN DISHES

HARISSA VEGGIE BOWL

THIS VEGGIE BOWL INCLUDES HOME-MADE HUMMUS MADE WITH ROASTED CARROTS –
YOU COULD INSTEAD REPLACE THE CARROTS WITH TOASTED WALNUTS OR AVOCADO.

INGREDIENTS

1 red pepper, deseeded and cut into wedges

1 yellow pepper, deseeded and cut into wedges

175 g/6 oz tenderstem broccoli

1 large red onion, peeled and cut into wedges

2 tsp gluten-free harissa paste

40 g/1½ oz hazelnuts

50 g/1¾ oz feta cheese (optional)

HUMMUS

175 g/6 oz carrots, peeled and thickly sliced

¼ tsp cumin seeds

3 tbsp olive oil

400 g/14 oz canned chickpeas, drained

1 garlic clove, roughly chopped

1 tbsp tahini

juice of 1 small lemon

salt and pepper (optional)

1. Preheat the oven to 200°C/400°F/Gas Mark 6.

2. To make the hummus, place the carrots in a roasting tin and sprinkle with the cumin seeds and ½ tablespoon of the oil. Roast in the preheated oven for 20–25 minutes until tender.

3. Meanwhile, arrange the remaining vegetables in a single layer in a separate large roasting tin. Mix the harissa paste with 1 tablespoon of the oil and sprinkle over the vegetables, then roast for 35 minutes. Add the hazelnuts after 20 minutes of cooking.

4. Place the cooked carrots in a food processor with the chickpeas and garlic and process until broken down. Add the tahini and lemon juice and process again until nearly smooth. Add the remaining oil, season to taste with salt and pepper, if using, and process for the final time.

5. Divide the hummus between four warmed bowls, then top with the roasted vegetables and hazelnuts and sprinkle with the cheese, if using.

PER SERVING : 327 KCALS | 20.7G FAT | 2.3G SAT FAT | 28.3G CARBS | 10.3G SUGAR | 9.4G FIBRE | 8.6G PROTEIN | 0.3G SALT

WINTER BLISS BOWL

A HEALTHY, CRUNCHY MAIN COURSE THAT IS FILLING AND FULL OF FIBRE FOR A HEALTHY DIGESTION. THIS IS THE PERFECT WAY TO 'EAT A RAINBOW', WITH A SPICY, HIGH-PROTEIN FALAFEL.

INGREDIENTS

220 g/7¾ oz white cabbage, shredded

220 g/7¾ oz red cabbage, shredded

1 small red pepper, deseeded and finely sliced

1 celery stick, finely sliced

1 carrot, peeled and grated

15 g/½ oz pomegranate seeds

20 g/¾ oz walnuts, roughly chopped

1 tbsp fresh parsley, roughly chopped

LEMON DRESSING

2 tbsp natural yogurt

juice of 1 lemon

1 tsp Dijon mustard

PATTIES

400 g/14 oz canned chickpeas, drained

1 tsp harissa paste

1 tbsp plain flour

½ tsp ground cumin

10 g/¼ oz fresh coriander

1 tbsp olive oil

salt and pepper (optional)

1. Place the white cabbage and red cabbage in a large bowl with the red pepper, celery, carrot, half the pomegranate seeds and half the walnuts and mix well to combine.

2. To make the lemon dressing, whisk together the yogurt, half the lemon juice and the mustard. Season to taste with salt and pepper, if using, and mix into the shredded vegetables.

3. To make the patties, place the chickpeas in a food processor along with the harissa paste, flour, cumin, coriander and the remaining lemon juice. Season to taste with salt and pepper, if using, and process until smooth.

4. Shape the mixture into eight patties.

5. Heat the oil in a frying pan, then add the patties and cook for 3–4 minutes on each side until golden.

6. Serve the patties with the colourful slaw, sprinkled with the remaining pomegranate seeds and walnuts and the parsley.

PER SERVING : 212 KCALS | 8.8G FAT | 1.1G SAT FAT | 26.5G CARBS | 13.3G SUGAR | 8.3G FIBRE | 7.3G PROTEIN | 0.2G SALT

MAPLE TOFU WITH EGG-FRIED RICE

TOFU IS A GREAT SOURCE OF VEGETARIAN PROTEIN, AND IS A VERSATILE INGREDIENT – IT CAN BE MARINATED BEFORE COOKING OR COOKED, AS HERE, IN A TASTY MAPLE SAUCE.

INGREDIENTS

1 egg

2 tsp sesame oil

3 tbsp coconut oil

200 g/7 oz long-grain rice, cooked

½ tsp ground turmeric

100 g/3½ oz frozen peas, thawed

4 spring onions, finely chopped

100 g/3½ oz beansprouts

50 g/1¾ oz cashew nuts

340 g/11¾ oz tofu, drained and dried on kitchen paper (drained weight)

3 pak choi, quartered lengthways

2 tbsp sesame seeds, toasted

MAPLE SAUCE

3 garlic cloves, crushed

3 tbsp gluten-free soy sauce

2 tbsp maple syrup

1 tbsp rice vinegar

1. Beat together the egg and sesame oil and set aside. Heat 2 tablespoons of the coconut oil in a wok or large frying pan, add the rice and turmeric and stir-fry for 3–4 minutes.

2. Add the peas, spring onions, beansprouts and cashew nuts and stir-fry for 3 minutes.

3. Push the rice to one side of the wok, pour in the egg mixture and leave to set for a few seconds, then move it around with chopsticks to break it up. Stir into the rice, then remove from the heat and cover while you cook the tofu.

4. Heat the remaining coconut oil in a frying pan, add the tofu and cook for 4–5 minutes, turning frequently, until lightly browned.

5. Mix the garlic, soy sauce, maple syrup and vinegar together, add to the tofu and cook, stirring occasionally, for 2–3 minutes, until the sauce thickens. Meanwhile, steam the pak choi.

6. Divide the rice between four warmed bowls, top with the pak choi and maple tofu, sprinkle with the sesame seeds and serve immediately.

PER SERVING : 614 KCALS | 29.4G FAT | 11.9G SAT FAT | 63.8G CARBS | 11.5G SUGAR | 6.87G FIBRE | 27G PROTEIN | 1.9G SALT

SWEET ROOTS BOWL

FULL OF STARCH AND SUGAR, ROOT VEGETABLES GIVE YOUR ENERGY LEVELS A LONG-TERM BOOST.
USING TAHINI IN DRESSINGS INCREASES YOUR INTAKE OF PROTEIN AND ESSENTIAL FATS.

INGREDIENTS

2 sweet potatoes, cut into chunks

2 beetroot, cut into chunks

2 red onions, cut into wedges

2 tbsp olive oil

2 tsp cumin seeds

75 g/2¾ oz brown rice

200 g/7 oz kale, shredded

2 tbsp flaked almonds, toasted

TAHINI DRESSING

4 tbsp gluten-free tahini

juice of 1 lemon

½ tsp pepper

½ tsp honey

1. Preheat the oven to 200°C/400°F/Gas Mark 6.

2. Place the sweet potatoes, beetroot and onions in a bowl with the oil and cumin seeds and toss together to coat with the oil.

3. Tip into a roasting tin and roast in the preheated oven for 35–40 minutes, until tender.

4. Meanwhile, cook the rice according to the packet instructions.

5. To make the dressing, whisk together the tahini, lemon juice, pepper and honey.

6. Stir the kale into the root vegetables 10 minutes before the end of the roasting time.

7. Drain the rice and divide between four warmed bowls.

8. Toss the vegetables with the dressing and serve on top of the rice, sprinkled with the toasted almonds.

PER SERVING : 402 KCALS | 18.4G FAT | 2.3G SAT FAT | 54.2G CARBS | 11.8G SUGAR | 9.5G FIBRE | 10.1G PROTEIN | 0.3G SALT

VEGGIE BURGER BOWL

THESE BURGERS ARE FILLING AND NUTRITIOUS – YOU COULD EAT THEM IN A BUN, BUT SERVING THEM IN A BOWL ON A BED OF COLOURFUL ROASTED RATATOUILLE IS JUST AS DELICIOUS.

25 mins, plus chilling

35–40 mins

4

INGREDIENTS

2 red peppers, deseeded and chopped

2 yellow peppers, deseeded and chopped

2 red onions, cut into wedges

2 courgettes, thickly sliced

3 tbsp olive oil

400 g/14 oz canned chickpeas, drained and rinsed

200 g/7 oz frozen peas, thawed

200 g/7 oz frozen sweetcorn, thawed

15 g/½ oz fresh coriander (including stalks)

¼ tsp cumin

80 g/2¾ oz plain flour

1 tbsp sunflower seeds

1 tbsp sesame seeds

salt and pepper (optional)

DRESSING

1 avocado, peeled, stoned and chopped

200 g/7 oz natural yogurt

2 spring onions, chopped

1 garlic clove, crushed

1 tbsp lime juice

salt and pepper (optional)

1. Preheat the oven to 200°C/400°F/Gas Mark 6. Place the red peppers, yellow peppers, onions and courgettes in a roasting tin and drizzle with 1 tablespoon of the oil. Roast for 35–40 minutes, until they are slightly charred at the edges.

2. Meanwhile, place the chickpeas, peas, sweetcorn, coriander, cumin and 70 g/2½ oz of the flour in a food processor and process to a thick paste. Add the sunflower seeds and sesame seeds, season with salt and pepper, if using, and process again to mix together.

3. Using wet hands, divide the mixture into four portions and shape each portion into a patty. Dust the patties with the remaining flour and chill in the refrigerator for 20 minutes.

4. Meanwhile to make the dressing, place the avocado, yogurt, spring onions, garlic and lime juice in a small blender and blend until smooth. Season to taste with salt and pepper, if using.

5. Heat the remaining oil in a frying pan, add the burgers and cook for 5–6 minutes on each side, until cooked through.

6. Divide the ratatouille between four bowls, top each one with a burger, then drizzle with the dressing and serve immediately.

PER SERVING : 534 KCALS | 24G FAT | 4G SAT FAT | 66G CARBS | 18.6G SUGAR | 15.8G FIBRE | 16.9G PROTEIN | 0.1G SALT

SWEET & SOUR 'STIR-FRY'

THIS ASIAN-INSPIRED BOWL IS FILLED WITH GOODIES – RAW KELP NOODLES ARE VERY LOW IN CARBS AND CALORIES, AND ORIENTAL MUSHROOMS CAN HELP REGULATE THE IMMUNE SYSTEM.

15 mins, plus sprouting and soaking

None

INGREDIENTS

40 g/1½ oz aduki beans suitable for sprouting

40 g/1½ oz mung beans suitable for sprouting

125 g/4½ oz parsnips, peeled and roughly chopped

125 g/4½ oz sweet potato, peeled and roughly chopped

1½ tbsp dried shiitake mushrooms, soaked in water for 15 minutes, drained and rinsed

200 g/7 oz raw kelp noodles

50 g/1¾ oz pak choi, sliced

50 g/1¾ oz enoki mushrooms

1 mild red chilli, deseeded and finely sliced

30 g/1 oz raw pine nuts

CHILLI SAUCE

1 small, medium–hot red chilli, deseeded and chopped

1 tsp peeled and chopped fresh ginger

1 tbsp raw coconut aminos

2 tsp raw agave nectar

1 tbsp cold-pressed extra virgin sesame oil

1 tsp raw tahini

juice of ½ lime

2 tsp raw rice vinegar

1. Start sprouting the aduki and mung beans 3 days before you want to make the stir-fry. Put the beans in a wide-necked glass jar and soak them overnight in tepid water, covered with muslin or a similar material. In the morning, drain and rinse the beans and fill the jar with fresh water. Drain and rinse them twice a day for 3 days, until they have sprouted. Rinse and drain to use.

2. For the sauce, process all the ingredients to create a paste. Add water until you have a thick pouring consistency and stir well.

3. Put the parsnips in a food processor and process until you have rice-sized pieces. Transfer to a mixing bowl. Do the same with the sweet potato and then lightly mix the two vegetables.

4. Chop the soaked shiitake mushrooms into small pieces and mix them into the vegetable rice.

5. Rinse the kelp noodles and shake to dry in a sieve. Arrange most of them in two serving bowls and add the vegetable rice.

6. Arrange the pak choi and enoki mushrooms on top of the rice, then dot spoonfuls of the sauce around the dish. Finish with the chilli slices, pine nuts and sprouted beans. Finally, arrange the remaining kelp noodles on top and serve.

PER SERVING : 489 KCALS | 19.2G FAT | 2G SAT FAT | 69.2G CARBS | 14.8G SUGAR | 14.1G FIBRE | 12.5G PROTEIN | 0.3G SALT

BLACK RICE & POMEGRANATE BOWL

THIS COLOURFUL BOWL IS BURSTING WITH PROTEIN-RICH BUTTER BEANS, BLACK RICE AND COTTAGE CHEESE. FULL OF GOODNESS, IT WILL HELP SUSTAIN YOUR ENERGY LEVELS.

INGREDIENTS

1 small butternut squash, deseeded and diced

1 red onion, peeled and sliced

1 tbsp olive oil

125 g/4½ oz black rice

70 g/2½ oz kale, shredded

2 tbsp pine nuts

1 x 400 g/14 oz can butter beans, drained and rinsed

4 tbsp cottage cheese, to serve

seeds from 1 pomegranate, to serve

TAHINI DRESSING

4 tbsp gluten-free tahini paste

juice of 1 lemon

1 garlic clove, crushed

2 tbsp extra virgin olive oil

1. Preheat the oven to 200°C/400°F/Gas Mark 6.

2. Place the butternut squash and onion on a roasting tray and drizzle with the olive oil. Roast in the preheated oven for 15 minutes.

3. Cook the rice according to the packet instructions.

4. Meanwhile, add the kale and pine nuts to the squash and roast for a further 10 minutes. Remove from the oven and toss in the butter beans.

5. To make the dressing, whisk the tahini, lemon juice, garlic and olive oil together in a small bowl. Set aside.

6. Drain the rice and divide between four warmed bowls. Spoon over the roasted vegetables and nuts, a dollop of cottage cheese and a sprinkling of pomegranate seeds.

7. Drizzle the dressing into each bowl to serve.

PER SERVING : 492 KCALS | 23.7G FAT | 3.3G SAT FAT | 58.7G CARBS | 10.7G SUGAR | 10.5G FIBRE | 14.8G PROTEIN | 0.2G SALT

LENTIL & AMARANTH TABBOULEH

AMARANTH IS A HIGH-QUALITY SOURCE OF PLANT PROTEIN. IT'S ALSO BURSTING WITH IRON AND CALCIUM, SO IT'S AN ESSENTIAL GRAIN TO HAVE IN YOUR KITCHEN.

INGREDIENTS

150 g/5½ oz amaranth

1 x 400 g/14 oz can green lentils, drained and rinsed

½ cucumber, diced

8 tomatoes, diced

1 small red onion, peeled and diced

15 g/½ oz fresh parsley, chopped

15 g/½ oz fresh mint, chopped

15 g/½ oz fresh coriander, chopped

100 g /3½ oz hazelnuts, toasted and chopped

150 g/5½ oz halloumi cheese, thickly sliced

salt and pepper (optional)

seeds from 1 pomegranate, to garnish

2 tbsp coconut flakes, to garnish

2 tbsp avocado oil, to serve

DRESSING

3 tbsp olive oil

1 tbsp balsamic vinegar

1 tsp wholegrain mustard

1 tsp honey

1. Cook the amaranth according to the packet instructions, until the grains are fluffy. Drain and leave to cool for a few minutes.

2. Meanwhile, make the dressing. Whisk the olive oil, vinegar, mustard and honey together in a bowl.

3. Place the amaranth in a large bowl with the lentils, cucumber, tomatoes, onion, herbs and hazelnuts. Pour over the dressing and toss together. Season to taste with salt and pepper, if using, and leave to stand at room temperature.

4. In a dry frying pan, cook the halloumi over a medium heat, until golden on both sides.

5. Serve the halloumi with the tabbouleh, garnished with pomegranate seeds, coconut flakes and a drizzle of avocado oil.

Hazelnuts are a good source of protein and monounsaturated fats. They are also rich in the antioxidant vitamin E.

PER SERVING : 727 KCALS | 47.1G FAT | 10.9G SAT FAT | 57.8G CARBS | 17.1G SUGAR | 12.8G FIBRE | 23.5G PROTEIN | 1.2G SALT

QUINOA CHILLI

QUINOA IS A SOUTH AMERICAN GRAIN THAT CONTAINS ALL NINE ESSENTIAL AMINO ACIDS. IT'S EASY TO COOK AND IS A GREAT, WHEAT-FREE REPLACEMENT FOR RICE OR COUSCOUS.

INGREDIENTS

50 g/1¾ oz red quinoa

1 tbsp olive oil, for sautéing

1 onion, peeled and diced

2 green chillies, deseeded and diced

1½ tsp smoked paprika

1 tsp chilli powder

2 tsp cumin powder

½ tsp cayenne pepper

2 garlic cloves, crushed

2 x 400 g/14 oz can chopped tomatoes

1 x 400 g/14 oz can kidney beans, drained and rinsed

1 x 400 g/14 oz can flageolet beans, drained and rinsed

100 ml/3½ fl oz water

15 g/½ oz fresh coriander leaves, chopped

2 tbsp frozen sweetcorn kernels, thawed

2 tbsp soured cream, to serve

1. Cook the quinoa according to the packet instructions.

2. Meanwhile, heat the oil in a separate large pan and sauté the onion over a medium heat for 3–4 minutes to soften.

3. Add the chillies to the pan and cook for 1 minute. Stir in the spices and garlic, and cook for 1 minute more.

4. Drain the quinoa and add to the pan along with the tomatoes, beans and water. Bring to a simmer and cook for 30 minutes, stirring occasionally, until thickened. Stir in half the coriander leaves.

5. Divide the chilli between four warmed serving bowls and scatter the sweetcorn kernels and remaining coriander over the top. Serve with the soured cream.

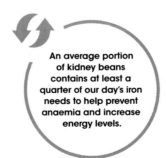

An average portion of kidney beans contains at least a quarter of our day's iron needs to help prevent anaemia and increase energy levels.

PER SERVING : 277 KCALS | 7.4G FAT | 1.3G SAT FAT | 38.6G CARBS | 10.5G SUGAR | 9.6G FIBRE | 12.3G PROTEIN | 0.1G SALT

ROAST CAULIFLOWER, KALE & CHICKPEA BOWL

THE SPICES IN THIS VEGGIE-PACKED BOWL ALL HAVE HEALTH PROPERTIES – GINGER IS SEEN AS A CURE-ALL, TURMERIC IS AN ANTI-INFLAMMATORY, AND CINNAMON HELPS STABILISE BLOOD SUGAR.

INGREDIENTS

1 tsp ground turmeric

1 tsp mustard seeds

½ tsp cumin seeds

½ tsp ground ginger

½ tsp ground coriander

½ tsp ground cinnamon

1 head of cauliflower, broken into florets

400 g/14 oz canned chickpeas, drained and rinsed

2 red onions, thickly sliced

2 tbsp olive oil

200 g/7 oz kale, shredded

100 g/3½ oz fresh wholemeal breadcrumbs

3 tbsp walnuts, chopped

2 tbsp flaked almonds

55 g/2 oz freshly grated Parmesan cheese

1. Preheat the oven to 200°C/400°F/Gas Mark 6.

2. Dry-fry the turmeric, mustard seeds, cumin seeds, ginger, coriander and cinnamon in a small frying pan for 2 minutes, or until the mustard seeds start to 'pop'.

3. Place the cauliflower florets, chickpeas and onion slices in a large roasting tin. Sprinkle with the spices and toss well together.

4. Drizzle over the oil and toss again.

5. Roast in the preheated oven for 20 minutes.

6. Stir the kale into the roast vegetables, and roast for a further 10 minutes, until the vegetables are tender and slightly charred.

7. Mix the breadcrumbs, walnuts and almonds and grated cheese together and sprinkle over the vegetables. Roast for a further 5–8 minutes, until they are golden.

8. Divide between four bowls and serve immediately.

PER SERVING : 406 KCALS | 19.5G FAT | 4.2G SAT FAT | 41.4G CARBS | 10.7G SUGAR | 12.2G FIBRE | 19.5G PROTEIN | 0.9G SALT

KIMCHI TOFU BOWL

KIMCHI IS A KOREAN PICKLE, USED TO ADD A SOUR, TANGY FLAVOUR TO FOOD – IT IS SAID TO BE GOOD FOR DIGESTION AND ALL-ROUND HEALTH.

20 mins, plus marinating

43-55 mins

INGREDIENTS

70 g/2½ oz brown basmati rice

70 g/2½ oz Camargue red rice

70 g/2½ oz wild rice

750 ml/1¼ pints cold water

3 tbsp mirin

1 tsp gluten-free soy sauce

2 tbsp miso paste

200 g/7 oz tofu, cut into triangles

1 tbsp coconut oil

2 red peppers, deseeded and sliced

4 spring onions, trimmed and sliced

2 courgettes, cut into matchsticks

1 carrot, cut into matchsticks

70 g/2½ oz shiitake mushrooms, sliced

70 g/2½ oz soya beans

50 g/1¾ oz beansprouts

4 tbsp kimchi

1. Rinse the rice thoroughly. Place in a saucepan with the water. Bring to the boil, then cover and simmer gently for 20–25 minutes, until cooked.

2. Meanwhile, mix the mirin, soy sauce and miso paste together and place in a non-metallic bowl. Add the tofu triangles, turning to coat with the marinade, then leave to marinate for 15–20 minutes.

3. Heat the coconut oil in a wok or large frying pan, add the red peppers and spring onions and stir-fry for 2–3 minutes, then add the courgettes and carrot and stir-fry for a further 3–4 minutes.

4. Add the mushrooms, soya beans, beansprouts, tofu and marinade. Stir-fry for 1 minute, then cover and steam for 2 minutes.

5. Drain the rice and divide between four warmed bowls. Top each portion with the stir-fry and 1 tablespoon of kimchi.

This recipe includes tofu, a good source of vegetarian protein, but you could use strips of chicken or prawns if you like.

PER SERVING : 423 KCALS | 11.4G FAT | 4.3G SAT FAT | 59.4G CARBS | 110G SUGAR | 8.7G FIBRE | 18.8G PROTEIN | 1.2G SALT

PROTEIN RICE BOWL

BROWN RICE ADDS IMPORTANT FIBRE AND FRESH CHILLI SUPPLIES A BIT
OF HEAT TO THIS PROTEIN-RICH VEGETARIAN LUNCH FOR TWO.

INGREDIENTS

150 g/5½ oz brown rice

2 large eggs

70 g/2½ oz spinach

4 spring onions, finely chopped

1 red chilli, deseeded and finely sliced

½ ripe avocado, sliced

2 tbsp roasted peanuts

VINAIGRETTE

2 tbsp olive oil

1 tsp Dijon mustard

1 tbsp cider vinegar

juice of ½ lemon

1. Place the rice in a large saucepan and cover with twice the volume of water. Bring to the boil and simmer for 25 minutes, or until the rice is tender and the liquid has nearly all disappeared. Continue to simmer for a further few minutes if some liquid remains.

2. Meanwhile, cook your eggs. Bring a small saucepan of water to the boil. Carefully add the eggs to the pan and boil for 7 minutes – the whites will be cooked and the yolks should still be very slightly soft. Drain and pour cold water over the eggs to stop them cooking. When cool enough to handle, tap them on the work surface to crack the shells and peel them. Cut the eggs into quarters.

3. Stir the spinach, half of the spring onions and a little red chilli into the cooked rice.

4. To make the vinaigrette, whisk the olive oil, Dijon mustard, cider vinegar and lemon juice together. Pour the dressing over the warm rice and mix to combine.

5. Divide the rice between two bowls and top each with the remaining spring onions, avocado, remaining red chilli, peanuts and egg quarters.

PER SERVING : 653 KCALS | 33.9G FAT | 5.9G SAT FAT | 71.1G CARBS | 4G SUGAR | 8.7G FIBRE | 19.1G PROTEIN | 0.3G SALT

SESAME SHRIMP WITH WATERMELON BOWL

THIS UNUSUAL COMBINATION REALLY DOES TASTE DELICIOUS – SUCCULENT, CRISP WATERMELON WITH RICH PRAWNS AND A CITRUS DRESSING. PERFECT FOR A SUMMER'S DAY.

INGREDIENTS

3 tbsp extra virgin olive oil

juice of 1 lime

1 garlic clove, crushed

550 g/1 lb 4 oz watermelon, peeled, seeded and sliced

40 g/1½ oz watercress

200 g/7 oz cooked king prawns

50 g/1¾ oz cashew nuts, toasted

2 spring onions, sliced

1 red chilli, sliced

2 tsp black sesame seeds

1. To make the dressing whisk together the oil, lime juice and garlic in a jug.

2. Divide the watermelon, watercress, prawns, nuts, spring onions, chilli and sesame seeds between two bowls.

3. Drizzle with the dressing to serve.

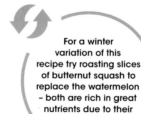

For a winter variation of this recipe try roasting slices of butternut squash to replace the watermelon – both are rich in great nutrients due to their vibrant colour.

PER SERVING : 544 KCALS | 34.1G FAT | 5.4G SAT FAT | 35.5G CARBS | 20.2G SUGAR | 3.2G FIBRE | 31G PROTEIN | 0.3G SALT

SALMON BURRITO BOWL

SALMON IS A GREAT SOURCE OF ESSENTIAL FATS AND PROTEIN. SERVED HERE WITH RICE AND BEANS, THIS RECIPE GIVES A REAL PROTEIN BOOST TO YOUR DAY.

20 mins | 30-33 mins | 4

INGREDIENTS

SALMON

1 tbsp coconut oil

2 garlic cloves, crushed

1 red onion, peeled and diced

1 celery stick, diced

1 red pepper, deseeded and diced

400 g/14 oz canned red kidney beans, rinsed and drained

200 g/7 oz long-grain rice

600 ml/1 pint vegetable stock

2 tbsp jerk paste

2 tbsp honey

4 salmon fillets, each weighing 150 g/5½ oz

MANGO SALSA

1 large mango, peeled, stoned and diced

½ red onion, finely diced

2 tbsp chopped fresh coriander

juice of 1 lime

1. To make the mango salsa, mix the mango, onion, coriander and lime juice together and leave to stand at room temperature.

2. Meanwhile, heat the coconut oil in a large saucepan, add the garlic, onion, celery and red pepper and sauté for 4–5 minutes. Add the kidney beans to the pan.

3. Add the rice and stock, bring to the boil, cover and simmer for about 15 minutes, until the rice is tender and the liquid has been absorbed.

4. Meanwhile, mix together the jerk paste and honey. Preheat the grill to hot and line a baking tray with foil. Place the salmon fillets on the prepared tray and spread the jerk mixture over each one.

5. Cook the salmon under the grill for 8–10 minutes, turning once.

6. Serve the rice in warmed bowls, topped with a fillet of salmon and some mango salsa.

If you can't get salmon, try using a white fish such as cod or haddock – both work well in this recipe.

PER SERVING : 716 KCALS | 26.2G FAT | 8.4G SAT FAT | 78G CARBS | 23.7G SUGAR | 7.7G FIBRE | 40.3G PROTEIN | 1.9G SALT

ONE-PAN SPICY CHICKEN

THIS DISH IS BASED ON THE GORGEOUS STEWS MADE IN MOROCCO, USING APRICOTS TO ADD SWEETNESS AND A COMBINATION OF SPICES FOR A FRAGRANT SAUCE.

INGREDIENTS

2 onions, peeled, 1 chopped and 1 sliced

100 g/3½ oz tomatoes, halved

3-cm/1¼-inch piece fresh ginger, peeled and chopped

3 garlic cloves, peeled

2 tbsp olive oil

4 x 150 g/5½ oz boneless, skinless chicken breasts, cut into bite-sized pieces

2 tsp ground cinnamon

1 tsp ground turmeric

2 tsp ground cumin

2 tsp ground coriander

1 large butternut squash, deseeded and cut into large pieces

50 g/1¾ oz dried apricots, halved

600 ml/1 pint gluten-free chicken stock

175 g/6 oz red quinoa

125 g/4½ oz feta cheese, crumbled

salt and pepper (optional)

15 g/½ oz fresh mint leaves, chopped, to garnish

1. Place the chopped onion in a blender with the tomatoes, ginger and garlic. Blitz to a paste.

2. Heat the olive oil in a large pan or casserole and cook the chicken over a medium heat for 4–5 minutes, until browned all over. Remove from the pan and reserve.

3. Cook the sliced onion in the same pan over a medium heat for 3–4 minutes. Stir in the spices and cook for a further minute. Stir the garlic paste into the pan and cook for 2 minutes.

4. Return the chicken to the pan with the squash, apricots and stock. Simmer for 15–20 minutes, until the chicken is cooked through. Season to taste with salt and pepper, if using.

5. Meanwhile, cook the quinoa according to the packet instructions.

6. Divide the chicken mixture and quinoa between four serving plates and sprinkle with feta and mint to serve.

PER SERVING : 656 KCALS | 21.6G FAT | 7.2G SAT FAT | 71.3G CARBS | 15.6G SUGAR | 10.9G FIBRE | 48.5G PROTEIN | 2.2G SALT

TURKEY, SESAME & GINGER NOODLES

TURKEY IS ONE OF THE LEANEST MEATS YOU CAN BUY AND AN INVALUABLE SOURCE OF PROTEIN. IT ALSO HAS A HIGH AMOUNT OF TRYPTOPHAN, WHICH CAN ACT AS A MOOD STABILIZER.

INGREDIENTS

150 g/5½ oz egg noodles

1 tbsp olive oil, for frying

2 garlic cloves, crushed

3-cm/1¼-inch piece fresh root ginger, peeled and diced

400 g/14 oz turkey breast, cut into strips

125 g/4½ oz mangetout

100 g/3½ oz broccoli florets

1 red pepper, deseeded and sliced

2 spring onions, trimmed and sliced

150 g/5½ oz beansprouts

1 tbsp sesame oil

1 tbsp gluten-free soy sauce

1 tbsp sweet chilli sauce

juice of ½ lime

100 g/3½ oz smooth, gluten-free peanut butter

100 g/3½ oz roasted peanuts, chopped

15 g/½ oz fresh coriander leaves, to garnish

1. Cook the egg noodles according to the packet instructions.

2. Heat the olive oil in a wok or large frying pan and add the garlic, ginger and turkey. Stir-fry over a medium heat for 3–4 minutes, until the turkey is cooked through. Remove from the pan and reserve.

3. Add the mangetout, broccoli and red pepper to the wok and stir-fry over a medium heat for 4–5 minutes. Add the spring onions and beansprouts, and continue to cook for 1 minute.

4. Whisk the sesame oil, soy sauce, chilli sauce, lime juice and peanut butter together in a small bowl and add to the wok along with the turkey and noodles. Toss together really well.

5. Divide the turkey and noodles between four warmed serving bowls and top with the peanuts and coriander to serve.

This dish is delicious eaten hot or cold. You can take any leftovers to work the next day for an easy lunch.

PER SERVING : 675 KCALS | 35.6G FAT | 6.2G SAT FAT | 50.2G CARBS | 11.5G SUGAR | 7.8G FIBRE | 44.2G PROTEIN | 1.3G SALT

PORK RAMEN
NOODLE BOWL

THIS RECIPE GIVES YOU TWO HEARTY BOWLS OF SPICY SOUP – FULL OF
FLAVOUR AND NUTRIENTS TO POWER YOU THROUGH THE DAY.

INGREDIENTS

800 ml/1¼ pints chicken stock

½ red chilli, deseeded and sliced

½ green chilli, deseeded and sliced

1 garlic clove, peeled and sliced

2.5-cm/1-inch piece fresh ginger, peeled and
cut into strips

1 small carrot, peeled and cut into batons

2 spring onions, sliced

300 g/10½ oz pork fillet, cut into strips

1 egg

125 g/4½ oz egg noodles

1 pak choi, sliced

pepper (optional)

sesame seeds, to garnish (optional)

1. Place the stock in a large saucepan and bring to a simmer.

2. Add the red chilli, green chilli, garlic, ginger, carrot and spring onion and simmer for 2 minutes.

3. Add the pork and continue to simmer for 5 minutes.

4. Meanwhile, bring a small saucepan of water to the boil. Add the egg and cook for 5 minutes. Drain and peel when cool enough to handle, then halve lengthways.

5. Add the egg noodles and pak choi to the pork mixture and cook for a further 3–4 minutes.

6. Divide between two warmed bowls and serve each portion with an egg half on top, sprinkled with pepper and sesame seeds, if using.

PER SERVING : 442 KCALS | 15.7G FAT | 5.7G SAT FAT | 23.3G CARBS | 7.3G SUGAR | 4.3G FIBRE | 43.8G PROTEIN | 4.5G SALT

MEXICAN BEEF & BEAN BOWL

CHILLI CON CARNE WITH EXTRA BEANS FOR PROTEIN AND FIBRE, PLUS RED PEPPERS FOR THEIR GREAT FLAVOUR – A PERFECT DISH TO MAKE IN ADVANCE AS THE FLAVOURS IMPROVE OVER TIME.

10 mins   20-25 mins   4

INGREDIENTS

1 tbsp olive oil

500 g/1 lb 2 oz fresh beef mince

1 onion, chopped

2 red peppers, deseeded and sliced

2½ tsp chilli powder

400 g/14 oz canned red kidney beans, drained

400 g/14 oz canned cannellini beans, drained

400 g/14 oz canned chopped tomatoes

1 tbsp tomato purée

100 ml/3½ fl oz gluten-free vegetable stock

200 g/7 oz basmati rice

2 tbsp chopped fresh coriander

2 tbsp soured cream

¼ tsp smoked paprika

salt and pepper (optional)

1. Heat the oil in a large frying pan, add the mince and cook for 2–3 minutes, until brown all over.

2. Add the onion and red peppers and cook, stirring occasionally, for 3–4 minutes.

3. Stir in the chilli powder and cook for 1 minute, then add the kidney beans, cannellini beans, tomatoes, tomato purée and stock. Bring to a simmer and simmer for 12–15 minutes. Season to taste with salt and pepper, if using.

4. Meanwhile, cook the rice according to the packet instructions.

5. Stir the coriander into the chilli and serve in warmed bowls with the rice, topped with a dollop of soured cream and a sprinkling of smoked paprika.

If you are vegetarian you can omit the mince altogether and make your chilli with beans and tomato sauce, adding lots of spice and chopped herbs for extra flavour.

PER SERVING : 682 KCALS | 25.4G FAT | 8.7G SAT FAT | 69.6G CARBS | 8.7G SUGAR | 11.3G FIBRE | 37.9G PROTEIN | 0.5G SALT

DESSERTS

CHOCOLATE GRANOLA WITH YOGURT

IF YOU LOVE CHOCOLATE YOU WILL LOVE THIS RECIPE – CREAMY LEMON CURD YOGURT, WITH FRESH BERRIES AND A HIT OF CHOCOLATE FROM THE FRESHLY MADE GRANOLA.

INGREDIENTS

50 g/1¾ oz pecan nuts, roughly chopped

25 g/1 oz pumpkin seeds

25 g/1 oz flaked almonds

15 g/½ oz desiccated coconut

25 g/1 oz cacao nibs

25 g/1 oz cashew nuts, roughly chopped

25 g/1 oz rolled oats

10 g/¼ oz cocoa powder

1 tbsp maple syrup

2 tbsp lemon curd

200 g/7 oz natural yogurt

175 g/6 oz strawberries, hulled and halved

125 g/4½ oz blueberries

100 g/3½ oz raspberries

100 g/3½ oz blackberries

few mint leaves, torn

zest of 1 lemon

1. Place the pecan nuts, pumpkin seeds, almonds, coconut, cacao nibs, cashew nuts, oats, cocoa powder and maple syrup in a bowl and mix well together.

2. Stir the lemon curd through the yogurt.

3. Divide the fruit between four bowls, top with the lemon yogurt, then spoon over the chocolate granola. Sprinkle with mint leaves and lemon zest to serve.

If you like a bit more 'crunch' to your granola, spread the granola mixture on a baking sheet and bake in the oven for 12–15 minutes at 180°C/350°F/ Gas Mark 4.

PER SERVING : 402 KCALS | 26.6G FAT | 7.7G SAT FAT | 36.6G CARBS | 19.1G SUGAR | 9.9G FIBRE | 10.9G PROTEIN | 0.1G SALT

BLACKBERRY & APPLE CRUMBLE

THIS DELICIOUS FRUITY DESSERT IS TOPPED WITH A NUTTY, OATY CRUMBLE.
THE HEDGEROW TASTE OF THE BLACKBERRIES IS BOOSTED WITH APPLES AND ORANGE JUICE.

INGREDIENTS

75 g/2¾ oz rolled oats

75 g/2¾ oz plain flour

50 g/1¾ oz pecan nuts

50 g/1¾ oz walnuts

25 g/1 oz sesame seeds

75 g/2¾ oz light muscovado sugar

125 g/4½ oz coconut oil

375 g/13 oz Bramley apples, peeled, cored
and thinly sliced

200 g/7 oz blackberries

juice of 1 orange

2 tbsp water

1½ tbsp caster sugar

4 tbsp skyr

4 tsp maple syrup

2 tbsp toasted flaked almonds, to serve

1. Preheat the oven to 180°C/350°F/Gas Mark 4.

2. Place the oats, flour, pecan nuts, walnuts and sesame seeds in a food processor and process until they resemble coarse crumbs. Add the muscovado sugar and coconut oil and process again.

3. Place the apples and blackberries in the base of a shallow ovenproof dish. Sprinkle over the orange juice and water, followed by the caster sugar.

4. Spoon over the crumble topping, then bake in the preheated oven for 25–30 minutes, until the top is golden and the fruit is bubbling around the sides.

5. Place the skyr in a bowl and drizzle over the maple syrup. Gently run a spoon through the skyr to give a marbled effect.

6. Divide the crumble between four bowls and serve with a dollop of the skyr and a sprinkling of toasted flaked almonds.

Most skyr yogurt is not made with animal rennet. If you are unsure, however, and follow a vegetarian diet, you can replace the skyr with coconut yogurt.

PER SERVING : 834 KCALS | 59.3G FAT | 27.1G SAT FAT | 81G CARBS | 43.8G SUGAR | 9.4G FIBRE | 12.1G PROTEIN | TRACE SALT

QUINOA FRUIT SALAD

QUINOA IS A GRAIN THAT MAKES A GREAT CRUNCHY ADDITION TO A
FRUIT SALAD. ADDING MINT AND GINGER ALSO ADDS A BIT OF SPICE.

INGREDIENTS

75 g/2¾ oz quinoa

400 ml/14 fl oz water

2 tsp date nectar or clear honey (use date
nectar for a vegan or raw option)

10 g/¼ oz dried cranberries

1-cm/½-inch piece fresh ginger, grated

6–8 fresh mint leaves, finely chopped

50 g/1¾ oz strawberries, hulled and halved

125 g/4½ oz honeydew melon, peeled,
deseeded and sliced

1 nectarine, cut into wedges

60 g/2¼ oz blueberries

1 tbsp toasted flaked almonds

1. Place the quinoa and water in a medium-sized saucepan and bring to the boil, then reduce the heat and cook for 8 minutes. Drain well, then spread over a foil-lined baking tray or grill pan.

2. Drizzle over the nectar and toast the quinoa under the grill for approximately 8 minutes until it starts to turn golden.

3. Tip the quinoa into a large bowl and stir in the cranberries, ginger and mint.

4. Toss in the strawberries, melon, nectarine and berries, then divide between two bowls, sprinkle with the almonds and serve.

Use fruits of your choice in this fruit salad – pick those in season for freshness. If you are not vegan this can be topped with a dollop of either yogurt or crème fraîche for a hint of creaminess.

PER SERVING : 280 KCALS | 5.1G FAT | 0.5G SAT FAT | 53.8G CARBS | 23.1G SUGAR | 6.5G FIBRE | 8.1G PROTEIN | TRACE SALT

RASPBERRY, CHIA SEED & PECAN POTS

CHIA SEEDS MAY BE TINY BUT THEY'RE PACKED WITH PROTEIN, FIBRE AND OMEGA-3 FATS.
IN ADDITION TO THE HEALTH BOOST, THEY GIVE JUICES AND PURÉED FRUITS GORGEOUS TEXTURE.

INGREDIENTS

400 g/14 oz raspberries

2 tbsp chia seeds

1 mango, stoned, peeled and chopped

400 g/14 oz Greek-style yogurt

3 kiwis, peeled and sliced

2 tbsp pecan nuts, toasted and roughly chopped, to decorate

1. Place the raspberries in a food processor and blitz until smooth, then place in a bowl. Stir in the chia seeds and leave to stand – the chia seeds will gradually thicken the mixture to a jam-like consistency.

2. Place the mango in a clean processor and blitz until smooth. Lightly stir through the yogurt, leaving trails of the mango showing.

3. Layer the yogurt, raspberry-chia mixture and kiwi slices in four glasses, finishing with yogurt on top.

4. Sprinkle the pudding with chopped pecan nuts to serve.

A mango is 14 per cent natural sugar, and this can be quickly converted into energy by the body. It is also rich in beta-carotene and vitamin C.

PER SERVING : 281 KCALS | 10.8G FAT | 4.1G SAT FAT | 37.7G CARBS | 23.2G SUGAR | 11.8G FIBRE | 12.8G PROTEIN | 0.1G SALT

PUMPKIN PIE SMOOTHIE BOWL

PUMPKIN PIE IS NORMALLY FULL OF SUGAR WITH A PASTRY BASE, BUT THIS
LOVELY BOWL OF GOODNESS MAKES A FILLING DESSERT OR BREAKFAST.

INGREDIENTS

800 g/1 lb 12 oz pumpkin or butternut
squash, peeled, deseeded and chopped

2 bananas, chopped

1 tbsp coconut oil

½ tbsp ground cinnamon

3 tbsp maple syrup

400 g/14 oz Greek-style yogurt

3 tbsp pumpkin seeds, toasted

2 tbsp sesame seeds, toasted

¼ tsp freshly grated nutmeg

1. Place the pumpkin in a saucepan with some water, bring to the boil, then simmer for 12–15 minutes, until tender.

2. Drain, return to the pan and add the bananas, coconut oil, cinnamon and maple syrup. Mash to a smooth consistency.

3. Divide between four bowls and top each one with a dollop of yogurt.

4. Sprinkle with the pumpkin seeds, sesame seeds and nutmeg and serve hot or cold.

PER SERVING : 341 KCALS | 14.8G FAT | 7.5G SAT FAT | 41.7G CARBS | 25.7G SUGAR | 3.3G FIBRE | 15.7G PROTEIN | 0.1G SALT

FRUIT & ALMOND MILK POWER BOWL

THIS BOWL SOAKS THE MUESLI OVERNIGHT – THIS HELPS START THE BREAKING DOWN PROCESS, MAKING IT EASIER TO DIGEST. IN-SEASON FRUIT WILL GIVE BETTER FLAVOUR AND RICHER NUTRIENTS.

15 mins, plus soaking

None

4

INGREDIENTS

250 g/9 oz rolled oats

55 g/2 oz raisins

55 g/2 oz ready-to-eat dried apricots, chopped

60 g/2¼ oz flaked almonds

2 dessert apples, grated

600 ml/1 pint almond milk

4 tbsp Greek-style yogurt

55 g/2 oz raspberries

55 g/2 oz strawberries

55 g/2 oz blueberries

4 tbsp maple syrup

2 tbsp cacao nibs

1. Mix the oats, raisins, apricots, almonds and apples together in a large bowl. Pour over the almond milk and mix well. Leave to soak overnight.

2. Divide between four bowls and top each portion with a dollop of yogurt, some raspberries, strawberries and blueberries, a drizzle of maple syrup and a sprinkling of cacao nibs.

For a quick version of this recipe, you could soak the muesli overnight, then just top with fresh fruit in the morning.

PER SERVING : 584 KCALS | 17.7G FAT | 3.9G SAT FAT | 97.2G CARBS | 41.8G SUGAR | 14.4G FIBRE | 14.8G PROTEIN | 0.2G SALT

PINEAPPLE POWER CHEESECAKE BOWL

ADDING TOFU TO THE CREAM CHEESE INCREASES THE PROTEIN CONTENT AND GIVES THIS CHEESECAKE A HEALTHY BOOST!

15 mins, plus chilling

2 mins

4

INGREDIENTS

200 g/7 oz tofu

200 g/7 oz cream cheese

2 tbsp maple syrup

grated rind of 1 orange

2 tbsp pecan nuts

400 g/14 oz fresh pineapple, peeled, cored and chopped

2 tbsp dry unsweetened coconut

2 tsp clear honey

8 sweet gluten-free oat cakes

1. Place the tofu, cream cheese, and maple syrup into a food processor and process until smooth.

2. Stir in the orange rind and divide the mixture among four small bowls. Chill in the refrigerator for 10 minutes.

3. Dry-fry the pecans, then coarsely chop.

4. Divide the pineapple among the bowls, then sprinkle with the chopped nuts and coconut.

5. Drizzle each bowl with a little honey.

6. Serve each portion with two sweet oat cakes.

The cheesecake base works for any fruit topping – try chopped strawberries and mint for a summer version, sprinkled with chopped plain chocolate for some decadence!

PER SERVING : 411 KCALS | 27.6G FAT | 13.8G SAT FAT | 33.6G CARBS | 20G SUGAR | 3.7G FIBRE | 9.3G PROTEIN | 0.7G SALT

HEALTHY FRUIT & NUT BOWL

THIS FRUIT AND NUT BOWL IS A DELECTABLE SUGAR-FREE TREAT! THE CHIA
SEEDS GIVE A JAM-LIKE CONSISTENCY, SO MAKE EXCELLENT FRUIT DESSERTS.

15 mins, plus chilling · None · 4

INGREDIENTS

1 orange

2 mangoes, peeled, stoned and chopped

4 tbsp chia seeds

4–5 tbsp milk

2 tbsp goji berries

seeds from 2 passion fruit

55 g/2 oz pineapple, cut into chunks

2 tbsp sunflower seeds

2 tbsp pumpkin seeds

55 g/2 oz redcurrants

2 kiwi fruit, peeled and sliced

2 tbsp flaked almonds, toasted

1. Grate the orange and reserve the rind, then peel the orange and put the flesh into a food processor with the chopped mango. Process for a few seconds to break everything down.

2. Add the orange rind, chia seeds and milk and process again for 20–30 seconds, scraping down any mixture from the side of the bowl. Leave to stand for 5 minutes.

3. Process the mixture again, then divide it between four bowls and chill in the refrigerator for 10 minutes.

4. Top with the remaining ingredients and serve.

This recipe has 4 tablespoons chia seeds, to serve 4. Stick to this quantity as it is not recommended that you have more than 1 tablespoon of chia seeds a day.

PER SERVING : 294 KCALS | 12G FAT | 1.3G SAT FAT | 44.6G CARBS | 29.9G SUGAR | 11.6G FIBRE | 7.8G PROTEIN | TRACE SALT

STRAWBERRY & RHUBARB SMOOTHIE BOWL

HERE IS A DELICIOUS CREAMY SUMMER DESSERT – ROASTED RHUBARB SMOOTHIE TOPPED WITH STRAWBERRY PURÉE AND SPRINKLED WITH FRESH FRUIT, NUTS AND CACAO NIBS.

INGREDIENTS

125 g/4½ oz rhubarb, cut into 2.5-cm/
1-inch pieces

1 tsp clear honey

125 g/4½ oz strawberries, hulled

150 g/5½ oz coconut yogurt

175 ml/6 fl oz coconut milk

1 tbsp cacao nibs

1 tbsp toasted flaked almonds

1 tsp chia seeds

1. Preheat the oven to 200°C/400°F/Gas Mark 6.

2. Place the rhubarb in a roasting tin and drizzle with the honey. Roast in the preheated oven for 12 minutes until soft. Leave to cool for 5 minutes.

3. Reserving two strawberries, place the remainder in a small blender and blend to a purée.

4. Transfer the rhubarb to a blender or food processor with the yogurt and milk and process until smooth.

5. Divide the smoothie between two bowls. Swirl the strawberry purée through each serving. Slice the remaining strawberries and place on top, then sprinkle with the cacao nibs, almonds and chia seeds.

If you don't have time to roast rhubarb, try a banana smoothie instead, using the same toppings, or even swap raspberries for the strawberry purée.

PER SERVING : 238 KCALS | 16.5G FAT | 11.8G SAT FAT | 19.7G CARBS | 10.1G SUGAR | 4.7G FIBRE | 4.1G PROTEIN | 0.1G SALT

CRANBERRY & RASPBERRY SMOOTHIE BOWL

SMOOTHIE BOWLS ARE NOT ONLY GREAT FOR BREAKFAST, THEY ALSO MAKE
PERFECT DESSERTS – LIGHT AND REFRESHING, BUT FULL OF FLAVOUR.

INGREDIENTS

50 g/1¾ oz cranberries (frozen or fresh)

200 g/7 oz raspberries

1 banana, sliced

400 ml/14 fl oz almond milk

1 small peach, stoned and sliced
into wedges

1 kiwi fruit, peeled, halved and sliced

1 tbsp pomegranate seeds

1 tbsp toasted flaked almonds

1. Put the cranberries, 150 g/5½ oz of the raspberries and the banana in a blender. Pour in the milk and process until smooth.

2. Pour into two bowls, top with the peach, kiwi fruit, the remaining raspberries, the pomegranate seeds and almonds and serve.

Cranberries
can be difficult
to find all year round,
but frozen ones are great
in this – and they keep
everything cool! You could
also top with a few dried
cranberries for added
cranberry flavour.

PER SERVING : 223 KCALS | 5.8G FAT | 0.2G SAT FAT | 42.5G CARBS | 22.1G SUGAR | 11.5G FIBRE | 5.2G PROTEIN | 0.3G SALT

NUTTY GRANOLA SUNDAES WITH YOGURT & MANGO

GRANOLA MAY BE MORE ASSOCIATED WITH BREAKFAST, BUT COMBINED WITH FRUIT AND YOGURT IT MAKES A REFRESHING DESSERT, OFFERING WELCOME ADDITIONAL TEXTURE AND CRUNCH.

10–15 mins · 35–40 mins · 6

INGREDIENTS

100 g/3½ oz whole almonds, roughly chopped

75 g/2¾ oz pecan nuts, roughly chopped

50 g/1¾ oz cashew nuts, roughly chopped

50 g/1¾ oz sunflower seeds

100 g/3½ oz pumpkin seeds

2 tbsp sesame seeds

125 g/4½ oz rolled oats

3 tbsp coconut oil

3 tbsp maple syrup

2 tsp ground cinnamon

100 g/3½ oz dried cranberries

8 tbsp Greek-style yogurt

1 mango, stoned, peeled and chopped

1. Preheat the oven to 180°C/350°F/Gas Mark 4.

2. Place the nuts in a large bowl with the seeds and oats, and mix well.

3. In a small pan, combine the coconut oil with the maple syrup and cinnamon over a medium heat. When the coconut oil has melted, remove from the heat and stir into the nut mixture, mixing well.

4. Spread the mixture over a baking sheet and bake in the preheated oven for 30–35 minutes, shaking and stirring from time to time, until golden.

5. Allow the granola to cool before stirring in the cranberries.

6. Divide the granola between six bowls and serve layered with yogurt and chopped mango.

The choice of nuts and seeds is up to you, but a wide variety is always best to gain the most nutrients available.

PER SERVING : 646 KCALS | 44.4G FAT | 10.9G SAT FAT | 52.6G CARBS | 25.9G SUGAR | 9.3G FIBRE | 19G PROTEIN | TRACE SALT

MIXED FRUIT SOUP BOWL

THIS SUMMERY COLD FRUIT SOUP IS PERFECT FOR A HOT DAY,
AND IS RICH IN ANTIOXIDANTS DUE TO ITS LOVELY BRIGHT COLOURS.

15 mins, plus chilling | None | 4

INGREDIENTS

2 papaya, peeled, deseeded and chopped

300 g/10½ oz strawberries, hulled

1 honeydew melon, deseeded, peeled and chopped

15 g/½ oz fresh mint leaves

1 tbsp stem ginger syrup

1 knob of stem ginger

100 g/3½ oz blueberries

1. Reserving 1 tablespoon of the chopped papaya, place the remainder in a food processor with 280 g/10 oz of the strawberries and process to a smooth purée.

2. Pour into a jug and chill in the refrigerator for 10 minutes.

3. Place all but 1 tablespoon of the chopped melon in the food processor with half the mint leaves, the ginger syrup and stem ginger. Process to a smooth purée. Pour into a jug and chill in the refrigerator for 10 minutes.

4. When you are ready to serve, divide each soup between four bowls, then use a knife to swirl them together. Drop a couple of ice cubes into each bowl.

5. Dice the reserved fruits and sprinkle over the soup, together with the blueberries and the remaining mint leaves.

PER SERVING : 173 KCALS | 0.9G FAT | 0.2G SAT FAT | 43.1G CARBS | 34.4G SUGAR | 5.7G FIBRE | 2.2G PROTEIN | 0.1G SALT

AÇAI POWER BOWL

AÇAI BOWLS ARE A POPULAR CHOICE FOR BREAKFAST AND DESSERT. THIS METHOD IS A TIME-SAVING WAY TO MAKE DAIRY-FREE ICE CREAM WITHOUT THE FUSS OF AN ICE-CREAM MAKER.

8 mins, plus freezing

8–10 mins

4

INGREDIENTS

2 bananas, sliced

300 g/10½ oz raspberries

100 g/3½ oz rolled oats

2 tbsp dried cranberries

1 tbsp sunflower seeds

3 tbsp maple syrup

100 ml/3½ fl oz non-dairy milk

1 tbsp açai powder

100 g/3½ oz blueberries

1. Place the banana slices and 200 g/7 oz of the raspberries in a single layer on a tray and freeze for at least 2 hours.

2. Preheat a grill to medium–hot. Mix the oats, cranberries, sunflower seeds and maple syrup together and spread over a baking sheet.

3. Cook under the preheated grill for 8–10 minutes, turning frequently, until golden (watch them carefully as they can suddenly burn). Leave to cool.

4. Meanwhile, place half the frozen banana in a food processor with half the frozen raspberries and half the milk. Process until broken down. With the machine running slowly add the açai powder and the remaining banana, raspberries and milk, adding enough milk to produce an ice cream consistency.

5. Divide the ice cream between four bowls, top with the blueberries and sprinkle with the maple-toasted oats.

PER SERVING : 279 KCALS | 4.5G FAT | 0.9G SAT FAT | 58G CARBS | 25.9G SUGAR | 10.1G FIBRE | 5.6G PROTEIN | TRACE SALT

INDEX

This edition published by Parragon Books Ltd in 2017
LOVE FOOD is an imprint of Parragon Books Ltd

Parragon Books Ltd
Chartist House
15–17 Trim Street
Bath BA1 1HA, UK
www.parragon.co.uk/love-food
www.parragon.com.au/love-food

ISBN 978-1-4748-8113-5

Printed in China

New recipes and introduction: Joy Skipper
New photography: Al Richardson
Editor: Emma Clegg

Additional images courtesy of iStock

NOTES FOR THE READER

This book uses both metric and imperial measurements.
Follow the same units of measurement throughout; do
not mix metric and imperial. All spoon measurements are
level: teaspoons are assumed to be 5 ml, and tablespoons
are assumed to be 15 ml. Unless otherwise stated, milk
is assumed to be full fat, eggs and individual fruits and
vegetables are medium, pepper is freshly ground black
pepper and salt is table salt. A pinch of salt is calculated
as $\frac{1}{16}$ of a teaspoon. Unless otherwise stated, all root
vegetables should be peeled prior to using.

The times given are an approximate guide only.
Preparation times differ according to the techniques used
by different people and the cooking times may also vary
from those given.

Please note that any ingredients stated as being optional
are not included in the nutritional values provided. The
nutritional values given are approximate and provided as
a guideline only, they do not account for individual cooks,
scales and portion sizes. The nutritional values provided
are per serving or per item.

Vegetarians and vegans should be aware that some of
the ready-made ingredients used in the recipes in this
book might contain animal products. Always check the
packaging before use.